Kings and Queens

Kings and Queens

The Plantagenets of England

By JANICE YOUNG BROOKS

THOMAS NELSON INC., PUBLISHERS
Nashville   New York

First edition

Library of Congress Cataloging in Publication Data
Brooks, Janice Young.
    Kings and queens.
    Includes index.
    1. Great Britain—Kings and rulers—Biography. 2. Great Britain—
History—Medieval period, 1066-1485.
I. Title.
DA177.B76   946'.00992   75-17843
ISBN 0-8407-6438-3

For Larry

Contents

Foreword

HISTORY *is* interesting. History teachers have been keeping that fact a secret from the general public for years, although a few curious outsiders have penetrated the secret, and some teachers, disloyal to the fraternity, have threatened to give it away from time to time. But it isn't fair to condemn the historians and teachers without giving them a fair hearing. They have kept the secret quite accidentally and out of the best of intentions. They seem to feel that to make history into History, a course worthy of scholastic attention, it must be dignified and formal and have an intellectual aura about it. These qualities usually add up to "dull." It is an educational philosophy that too often removes human nature from the story of human endeavor.

That is all that history really is—the story of human endeavor. After all, birth, death, love, and hate are seldom dignified, but they are real and they are generally more gripping than political philosophy or national trends. It is difficult to get fired up about the Magna Carta, for example, unless you are personally acquainted with the cruel and hedonistic King John, whose behavior made the Magna Carta necessary.

Kings and Queens is made up of the "good parts," which the scholars all know about but leave out of the textbooks because they are too personal, too trivial, or too earthy to fit in with dignity. This is why I have included works of good historical fiction in the bibliographies. Good historical fiction is the kind that adheres scrupulously to the known facts and fills in the unknown gaps with plausible actions and conversations. Some of the books listed do not feature the king as a main character but show what effect his personality had on other people living at the time. Historical fiction is the best way to start learning history. It opens the door to scholarly history books. Once you know an historical figure personally, you may find yourself charging eagerly through the kind of weighty old volumes that were previously useful only for pressing flowers or propping doors open.

This book is a cause—history for people who hate history. It is a very personal and informal introduction to some highly interesting people who happen to have been the main characters of five hundred years of English history. The book can also serve as a reference point for people who are already sold on history but find it hard to keep all the Henrys and Edwards and Richards straight. The English are rather unimaginative at nicknaming monarchs. No student of French history could confuse Philip the Fair with Saint Louis. Nor do Spanish scholars have trouble placing Juana the Mad or Pedro the Cruel. But only two English kings, William the Conqueror and Richard the Lionhearted, are always known by name rather than numeral. The concept of nicknaming the others is tempting. Henry the Undecided and Henry the Stingy would be far easier to remember than Henry III and Henry VII.

Whatever names they are given, the medieval English monarchs are fascinating people. They represent the full scope of human characteristics and motivations. Today the English monarchy is little more than an ornament on the fabric of British politics, but in the Middle Ages the king and queen *were* England. Their behavior and personality determined whether England had war or peace, poverty or prosperity, glory or tragedy. Their history, then, is the history of their land and their people.

J. Y. B.

CHAPTER I

The Pre-Plantagenets

1065

ALTHOUGH human nature has an obstinate tendency
to remain much the same through centuries, the standards
by which it is judged vary widely. Therefore, before meeting and judging William the Conqueror, it is necessary
to know something about the England of 1065, before
William became the Conqueror.

In 1065 England was inhabited by an Anglo-Saxon
people whose king was a vacuous individual named
Edward. In later years his impotence and almost total
absence of personality would be interpreted as saintliness,
and he would be remembered as Edward the Confessor or
in some circles as Edward the Simple. Edward's precarious
hold on his medieval throne was due to the strength and
skill of his wife's family, especially that of his brother-in-
law, Harold Godwinson, an able and energetic man in
his early forties. Harold was an experienced military
leader and had been a wise adviser to the saintly Edward,
whose idea of military activity was to run about blindly
slaughtering everything in sight.

King Edward became ill in December of 1065 and died

on January 5, 1066. The witenagemot then elected Harold king.

The witenagemot has been called a Saxon version of Parliament, though the similarity was slight. One of its duties was to elect a new king when an old king died. On such an occasion the witenagemot was a loose organization that seemed to consist mainly of anyone important who happened to be left standing around court. In practice, the monarchy was hereditary, though in theory the witenagemot was not obligated to elect the next of kin. But since the witenagemot had always been made up of supporters of the king, it generally elected his chosen successor.

In Edward's case, however, it was difficult to determine whom he favored. He had no children, and although he had appeared to favor Harold to fill his place, Edward had indiscriminately promised the crown to a number of people. One of them was William of Normandy.

William's claim to the English throne also involved an oath. Medieval society functioned almost exclusively by the spoken word. Literacy was a rare commodity and was not regarded as an especially valuable asset. In fact, the ability to read and write was generally limited to clerks. Those in positions of importance who learned to read considered it a convenience, not a mark of intellectual capacity. A modern equivalent might be the ability to take shorthand, a necessary and useful skill certainly, but not a creative process. Since there were few legal contracts in writing, the taking of oaths became a complicated and important system.

There were, of course, varying degrees of obligation then attached to oaths. A simple "I promise" was about as important then as now and depended on the personal scruples of the individual. A religious oath, "I swear before God," carried a spiritual obligation and was more binding, although the Deity was expected to overlook certain transgressions if circumstances demanded it.

The highest level of oath was that sworn on holy relics, which were in abundant supply. To make an oath while holding a bone of Saint Peter or a splinter of the Holy Cross was to be completely committed. Not only was a holy oath a social agreement which, if broken, could cause the oath taker to be shunned by his peers, it was also a weighty burden on the soul. Unfulfilled, it could condemn the oath breaker to eternal damnation.

The role of the witenagemot and the legality of a certain oath were to be important factors in the Norman Conquest of Anglo-Saxon England.

William the Conqueror
1027–1087

HIS few friends called him William of Normandy; his unwilling subjects called him William the Bastard; history calls him William the Conqueror.* He was so vicious that he sometimes shocked even his contemporaries in an age when brutality was the norm. He also had a genius for organization that verged on the pathological.

William was born in what is now France about 1027.

------

* No one dared call him the Conqueror to his face. He claimed that he was the rightful king and that the Conquest was only the means of ensuring his right.

His mother was Arlette, a girl from Falaise, whose father was the village tanner and embalmer. William's father was Robert, Duke of Normandy.

William was illegitimate. In fact, illegitimacy was something of a tradition in Duke Robert's family. Robert did marry a woman of his own class, but she never gave him any children, so William remained Robert's heir. When William was about seven years old, Duke Robert decided to go on a Crusade. He went trudging off in his pilgrim's robe and was never heard from again. He was logically assumed to be dead, and his bastard child became Duke of Normandy.

Holding on to a rich inheritance in spite of the double disadvantages of youth and illegitimacy created a keen sense of survival in the young William of Normandy. Little is known of his youth, but there could have been no time for childish frivolities with his life and title in danger of seizure by his ambitious relatives. But William was ambitious too, and with the support of the king of France, he managed to keep his dukedom and his head.

When he judged it necessary to have a wife, William decided on Matilda of Flanders, the daughter of Baldwin V of Flanders, who was reputedly the richest man in Europe. At one time, Matilda had been infatuated with a fair young Saxon lord named Brithric. Unfortunately for Brithric, he turned Matilda down, and she never forgot it.

Meanwhile, William offered himself as a prospective son-in-law to Baldwin, who favored the plan, but Matilda had no inclination to marry a prominent bastard, and she said so. Gracious acceptance of defeat was not one of William's outstanding features. He reacted to Matilda's rejection with characteristic violence. The popular version of the story is that when he came upon her riding through town, he yanked her off her horse, rolled her around in the mud, and administered a few kicks before haughtily riding off. Oddly enough, Matilda was favorably impressed by this ungentlemanly assault and changed her mind about marrying him. Of course, William had something of an advantage in that Matilda was only slightly over four feet tall.

In spite of their tavern-brawl-type courtship, William and Matilda seemed to have been in accord thereafter. Though of minute stature, Matilda was not of a retiring nature. She handled Normandy while William was overpowering England, and when, after the Battle of Hastings, her old flame Brithric's extensive holdings were confiscated, she saw to it that Brithric ended up in a dungeon, where he died. His lands were put in Matilda's name.

Though there were long separations, William never seemed to have the time or the inclination to take a mistress. Matilda did hear rumors of a dalliance once on William's part, and she had the lady in question hamstrung, then put to death. Matilda was not to be trifled with.

William had apparently conceived a desire to be king of England long before he had the opportunity. His great-grandfather was Richard I of Normandy, who was also the grandfather of Edward the Confessor, so William was a cousin to the king. Some years before Edward's death, William had taken advantage of a temporary absence of the obstreperous Godwin family (including Harold) to visit King Edward. William could be quite charming, and the dull-witted monarch was so impressed with his fast-talking cousin that he promised him the crown. Or so William claimed.

The second boon to William's ambitions began with a literal ill wind for Harold. One day in 1065, while crossing the Channel, Harold's ship was blown off course, and he ended up in Normandy. William turned on the charm again and entertained him royally but for such a long time that it became clear that Harold, instead of being a guest, was a well-treated prisoner. Every time Harold started making a polite move to leave, William planned a new feast or hunt in honor of his guest. Eventually, William suggested that Harold promise to support William's claim to the throne. By this time, Harold was sick of Normandy and its duke, and making a few empty promises seemed a small price to pay to secure his release from the enforced hospitality.

The proper ceremony was arranged for making the pledge, and it was carried out to everyone's satisfaction. Not until after Harold had sworn his oath was the cover removed from the table on which he had rested his hands and the hidden relics were revealed. It was a bad moment for Harold, who must have realized that if he broke this holy oath, the Pope's support would probably go to William.

Harold went back to England, and in December of 1065, King Edward became ill. He died the first week in January, and the witenagemot immediately elected Harold as king. Harold appreciated the importance of the oath he had taken in Normandy, but he accepted the crown in spite of it. One of his reasons for doing it was personal ambition. Harold was a practical man who saw the oath incident as nothing more than a dirty trick. He probably had no fear of spiritual consequences, and more important, he felt that England needed him. He had been running things well for the muddle-headed King Edward for some time, and the fact that the witenagemot had elected him in spite of the complete absence of royal blood in his veins indicated that they recognized his abilities.

Harold's election in January initiated a year of feverish activity on several fronts. When the news reached Normandy, William staged a brief but virulent tantrum, then got busy organizing an invasion. William was always terrifyingly well organized. He persuaded the Normans to give support by promising them land, titles, and heiresses, which were the usual spoils of war, and cool-headed William had it all put down in a ledger, noting what each had promised to supply and what he was to get in return. By August, William had built, borrowed, and recruited a fleet of over five hundred ships and an army of seven thousand men.

But even William couldn't organize nature. For weeks the entire group sat and waited impatiently for a good wind so they could sail across the Channel. When they finally landed, there didn't seem to be anyone to fight. The local inhabitants had prudently fled, and Harold was busy beating off other armed claimants to his throne at several other points in the kingdom. This spread men and morale pretty thin. From Harold's point of view, William was just one of his problems.

Harold was returning from a victory in the north of England when William landed in the south. Harold led his men to the small fishing village of Hastings, where William's troops were waiting, and on October 14, 1066, the most important battle in English history was fought. It appeared for some time that Harold might be the victor. Then William's troops staged a mock retreat, and Harold's front lines went jubilantly charging after them. With a break now in the tight front resistance, William's troops

turned and charged back into the Saxons. Some anony-
mous archer loosed an arrow that pierced Harold's eye.
He died in moments. The Norman Conquest was over.
Harold's mistress came to the battlefield later to identify
the body.

William was crowned on Christmas Day, 1066, less than
a year after Edward the Confessor's death. William was
now officially king of England, but it would be a mistake
to believe that the Saxons were a bunch of sheep who
docilely flocked to his standard. Besides, William wasn't
content to be a nominal king; he wanted to be all-power-
ful dictator over a land totally submissive to him. He
spent the next twenty years trying to get everyone under
control. He and his Norman adherents were there to stay,
but the Saxons considered them alien usurpers. Many
generations went by before the Normans were assimilated,
and it took three hundred years after that for English,
the native tongue, to replace Norman French as the
language of the court.

William believed in the steamroller approach to running a country. He felt that the best way to subdue an
area was to obliterate it. In cases of rebellion, he sent in
his men to burn the houses, fields, and orchards. They
killed all the livestock and as much of the populace as
possible. When William's men departed, there was never
anything left. A man whose starving family is hiding in
a cave or forest isn't likely to leave them and go fight his
overlord's battles. If one can put moral consideration
aside, as William was in the habit of doing, it was a very
practical and thorough way of dealing with rebellion.

Early in 1068, William was well enough entrenched to
summon Matilda and their children to England. He had
left Matilda to rule Normandy jointly with their oldest

son, Robert, who was her favorite. They had several children by that time. Robert was then fourteen. He had been followed by Richard, who died young, William, who was called Rufus because of his florid complexion, and five sisters. Late in the year of her arrival in England, Matilda gave birth to a boy named Henry, who would later become the first king of this new line to be born on English soil.

Like many kings, William expected his sons to do much to support him, but he was too jealous of his power to share authority with them. He and his son Robert were constantly at odds. Robert had few of his father's skills and was openly impatient for William's death. They became so antagonistic that they eventually got into a private battle. Robert managed to knock William off his horse and was at the point of killing him when one of William's friends (he did have some) dashed into the fray and hoisted the armor-clad king back into his saddle. That was something of an accomplishment, because in addition to the heavy armor, William himself was getting quite paunchy. His stomach was so fat that once, when he was confined to bed with an illness, the king of France commented that it was obvious that William was having a baby. William was not amused.

William realized that the country he had conquered had more potential wealth to offer than was coming into the royal pocket. But he had no way of knowing just where it was hiding, for nobody really knew much about England as a whole. So William sent out an army of clerks to take a census. The census was to tell exactly who owned what, including land, serfs, grain, cattle, sheep—anything that could conceivably be taxed. The resulting mass of information was the Domesday Book. Now

William knew precisely where he could most profitably apply the screws. His Norman mercenaries, who had been so generously rewarded with lands and titles, now began to pay for them. The dispossessed Saxons enjoyed this turn of events.

From time to time, there were rebellions in Normandy. William was sacking the town of Mantes as a result of one flare-up in 1087 when his horse stepped on a hot coal and threw him against the pommel of the saddle. He was ill with severe abdominal pains for six weeks before he died. He may have had internal injuries, but it is more likely that the accident coincided with an appendicitis attack.

William seems to have been afflicted by a fit of virtue at the end, because he admitted that he had a few sins on his soul. He assigned Normandy to his son Robert and England to William Rufus. To Henry, his youngest, he bequeathed a large sum of money. Then on September 9, 1087, he died. Armed aggression had been his life style; he had lived and died by it.

His funeral was distressingly anticlimactic. Only after the services were under way did they discover that his corpulent body didn't fit the sarcophagus. The priests tried to cram it in anyway, and in the process, the great rotten belly burst. The services were concluded in undignified haste while the guests ran, retching, from the building.

William Rufus
1056 (?) –1100

WILLIAM Rufus is one of the most interesting and least remembered villains in English history. He was a tough, vain little man with curly blond hair, his father's fat stomach, and an overwhelming affection for money and power. Most of what we know about him comes from the records kept by monks. They were inclined to portray him unsympathetically for several reasons.

First, Rufus made no pretense of being on friendly terms with his Maker. He was of the opinion that he and God had a mutually antagonistic relationship. Once, when he had gotten over a near-fatal illness, it was suggested that he thank God for his recovery. He said he saw no reason to thank God for making him well because it was God that had made him sick in the first place. Another occasion for blasphemy involved a trial by boiling water. People believed that if the defendant survived, it meant that the Lord recognized his innocence. Several men were arrested for killing a deer in the royal forest. When they came through the boiling-water trial unscathed, Rufus churlishly announced that God was obviously mistaken and that next time he would take matters in his own hands and leave God out of it.

The other reason for his unpopularity was money. Rufus loved it. He had no scruples about relieving everyone, including the Church, of as much of it as possible. Rufus had a lot of help from a monk by the name of Ralph Flambard, who had a genius for finding legal ways of robbing the rich to give to the king. Ralph declared that the king was everybody's heir. When a man died, all his property—land, money, marriageable daughters— was automatically willed solely to the king. The king usually sold the land back to the real heir for his lifetime. After that it again reverted to the Crown.

With Ralph's help, Rufus next turned his greedy attention to the Church. Whenever the head of an abbey died, the king had the privilege of appointing a successor, and the unholy pair fell on the fact that during the interval all the revenues came to the king. Rufus did the obvious; he then simply ceased to appoint people to fill the vacancies. That way, every penny that found its way into the Church ended up in Rufus' pocket. He did make a few appointments when the appointee was willing to pay enough, and on one occasion he even gave one appointment away to spite the two greedy monks who were trying to outbid each other for a position.

The English complained that Rufus was too critical and harsh in dealing with them. Actually, that was only partly true. He *didn't* like the English, but he didn't much care for anyone else either, and if he was hard on his own subjects, it was only because they were close at hand. His reign was a series of wars, rebellions, quarrels, and battles, none of which is worth recounting individually, for nothing important ever came of them. Most of the fights were family affairs between Rufus and his brothers: Robert, who had inherited Normandy and let it go entirely to ruin, and Henry. Rufus was also on bad terms with Wales and Scotland. Most of his military campaigns were intelligently planned and well organized, but after mildly successful beginnings, they always petered out because Rufus had lost interest.

Rufus was the only adult bachelor king that England was to have for many centuries. He had no mistresses or illegitimate children, another record that was unchallenged by his successors for a long time. Up until Rufus' time the barons were primarily fighting machines. They wore practical, fitted clothing that went under armor easily, and they had short hair and clean-shaven faces, so their enemies had fewer means of getting a good grip on them in hand-to-hand combat. But Rufus spent a great deal of the money he wrung from the barons and the Church in lavish personal spending on clothes, and the young dandies in his court went in for long curling hair, flowing floor-length coats, and fancy pointed shoes. The older crowd considered the young set a degenerate group of effeminate fops, which was a pretty accurate assessment.

In spite of his greed, Rufus liked to be generous—publicly, grandly, senselessly. He didn't care anything for the value of the causes to which he gave, so long as he could make a great show of giving. The spirit of chivalry was beginning to take hold, and Rufus was an adherent of the code so long as it was convenient. He was even known to have kept a few promises. As one of his biographers points out, the standards of chivalry were poor standards, but they were slightly better than no standards at all.

William Rufus died in 1100 at the age of forty. All that is certain is that he went hunting one afternoon in the New Forest with a group that included his young brother Henry. The group split up, and Rufus with one companion went off on his own. He was found dead hours later with an arrow in his chest. The companion was gone.

Each monk who recorded the incident described it differently and in great detail, although they agree that there were no witnesses. One story was that the companion (they can't agree who he was) shot Rufus deliberately, then fled. Another says Rufus had the sun in his eyes and accidentally stepped into the path of an arrow that had been aimed at a stag. The companion fled for fear he wouldn't be believed. Another monk said that the arrow ricocheted off a tree and hit Rufus. Yet another story has Rufus tripping and falling on an arrow, stuck point uppermost in the ground for some unexplained reason. The most picturesque version has the arrow heading straight for the aforementioned stag when Satan sticks an arm out of nowhere, grabs the arrow, and flings it at Rufus. None of these writers suggests the obvious possibility, that Henry, who had the most to gain, was responsible. After all, they were writing during Henry's reign.

At any rate, Rufus was beyond setting the record straight by the time he was found, and a convenient dung cart was appropriated to haul the body back to Winchester. A hasty burial followed, and Henry declared himself king.

There was only a halfhearted attempt to investigate the agency of Rufus' death. No one much cared who had done it. Apparently, it was such a relief to be rid of the fat little tyrant that his death was regarded as a good thing that shouldn't be looked into too closely.

Henry I
1068–1135

HENRY I was a one-man population explosion. He acknowledged at least twenty illegitimate children by nearly as many different women. A contemporary historian assures us that he did not engage in these affairs for pleasure. Certainly not! His only motive for intimacy was to beget children. That prim chronicler neglects to explain what Henry wanted with a couple of dozen bastards. Despite that, Henry's behavior was considered a model of virtue in comparison with the moral climate of the previous court.

Henry I was the fourth son of William the Conqueror. He was born in England two years after the Conquest. William had left his lands to Henry's two older brothers (one of the four sons having died young) and a sum of money to Henry. Henry used the money to buy a small section of France, which he ruled very well until his brothers got together and took it away from him. The oldest brother, Robert, had decided to go crusading, and he financed the trip by pawning Normandy to Rufus. Rufus died before Robert's return, but Robert always regarded Normandy as still belonging to him. He felt it was just out on loan. Henry knew that his bubble-headed older brother would never scrape together enough money to reclaim Normandy, so he considered the duchy part of his inheritance. In either case, Robert had still been off on his Crusade when Rufus died, so he had nothing to say about Normandy's fate at the time.

Henry had been in the hunting party the day Rufus mysteriously met his well-deserved end in the New Forest. When Henry got word of Rufus' death, he made tracks for the royal treasury. It was there that the barons found him, engaged in a sword fight with the treasurer, who refused to turn the keys to the treasury over to him until someone declared him king. The council sat down to decide between Henry and Robert. There were arguments on both sides. Some of the barons were in favor of Robert because he was a nitwit, under whose rule they could get away with anything. Henry's advantage was his English birth and his physical presence. The common people of England preferred Henry because he had been born in England. It made him seem a little less alien in their eyes than the Conqueror's older son. While the council was meeting, a crowd gathered outside the castle walls and made it known that if the council didn't appoint Henry, they would tear the place down. The council appointed Henry.

Henry's coronation was held a few days later, on August 5, 1100, and he not only swore to undo the wrongs of Rufus' reign, he had a charter drawn up that specifically listed those wrongs. The charter diminished the tyrannical power that William the Conqueror and William Rufus had wielded. It wasn't that Henry was anxious to have less power; the charter was not an indication of political idealism on Henry's part—it was a measure designed to appease the barons and to strengthen Henry's support. His position was still shaky when it became known that Robert was on his way back. No one could predict what Robert would try to do when he heard of Henry's assumption of power.

Henry did adhere somewhat to the spirit if not to the letter of the charter. He was the first of the Norman rulers to whom the ultimate power was secondary to peace.

Another of Henry's first acts was of minor importance but was regarded by many as encouraging. He locked up Rufus' disreputable crony Ralph Flambard in the newly completed White Tower (the central part of the Tower of London). Unfortunately, this first prisoner of that famous prison was also its first escapee.

The first few months of Henry's reign were the busiest. As soon as the coronation was over, he decided to remedy his single — though obviously not lonely — state. The young woman he wanted to marry had an interesting background. Her name was Eadgyth or Edith (spelling in those days was a slapdash system, subject entirely to the writer's whim). Her father had been Malcolm, the king of Scotland who dethroned the real-life Macbeth. When

Malcolm died, a belligerent brother of his, Donald Bane, came to the throne, and Malcolm's family had to flee. Edith's mother was Margaret, a relative of Edward the Confessor. The English so revered Margaret that they were happy to consider her lovely daughter Edith more English than Scottish.

Edith was a very good choice for Henry, but there was a problem. She and her sisters had been put in a nunnery for their safety, and their overbearing aunt had insisted that Edith become a nun. The plan hadn't impressed Edith. She couldn't see herself leading a long life of chastity and seclusion.

A council of churchmen was called to question her as to her status. She explained that she had worn the veil of a nun only in her aunt's presence, but had not taken any religious vows. One version of the story has her donning the veil only to repulse an amorous advance by Rufus. In light of that gentleman's sexual eccentricities the story is hardly believable.

The council decided in favor of Edith and declared her free to take an earthly bridegroom. She changed her name to Matilda in honor of Henry's mother, and they were married in November of 1100. She was twenty, he thirty-one. Surprisingly enough, Henry was faithful to her, at least for several years.

Matilda came to be known as Good Queen Mold—Mold (Maud) being a medieval nickname for Matilda and not an indication of a mildewed condition. She was both generous and practical. She contributed to the building of churches, which was a traditional activity for queens, and she financed such purely practical things as roads, bridges, and hospitals.

Robert had returned to Normandy a month after

Henry's accession. At first he had done nothing. He was lazy and pleasure loving and was content to leave things as they were, but some of the barons in Normandy, who had grown fat and rich under his lenient rule, wanted to extend his holdings to include England.

Robert was easily swayed, and in 1102 he invaded England. He wasn't doing too badly and might even have won, but Henry bought him off. Robert had a highly developed talent for running through money. He had already frittered away his wife's large inheritance and the loan from Rufus. He gladly pocketed Henry's bribe and went home.

Henry realized that Robert would run out of money again. Since he didn't want to face years of bribing Robert at regular intervals, he invaded Normandy in 1105. He crushed the rebellious barons and captured Robert, who was taken to England, where he spent the remaining twenty-nine years of his life confined at Cardiff Castle.

Henry could now settle down to applying his talents to governing rather than fighting. Henry was a hard-working and intelligent administrator with a sincere interest in fairness for which he earned the designation "Lion of Justice." His methods were severe but efficient, and he created for the first time in English history a sense of unity in the island. In dealing with his subjects, he didn't distinguish between Norman Englishmen and Saxon Englishmen. Both were treated the same way, and they began to regard each other with a little less antagonism.

Henry I was known by later ages as Henry Beauclerc, which implies a scholarly turn of mind that he really didn't possess. He could read and write Norman French, his everyday language. (Rufus had never bothered to learn to read or write at all, so Henry shines in comparison.) He could also read some Latin and could even speak a smattering of English, which was considered by the nobility to be about as cultured as pig latin. He didn't learn English for pleasure or any sort of intellectual fulfillment. He simply saw it as a practical aid of ruling.

Life proceeded on an even keel for Henry. Matilda had given birth to a son, William, in 1103, and a daughter, Alice, in 1104 (Henry later changed her name to Matilda, too). Then, in 1118, Matilda died and her death marked the beginning of the decline of Henry's fortunes.

In the winter of 1120, the royal family and the court were returning to England from a visit to Normandy. Henry came ahead, and Prince William and the rest of the young people were to follow on a ship called *Blanche Nef* (the White Ship). The young people got drunk and rowdy, and when the drunkenness extended to the crew, the *Blanche Nef* struck a reef and quickly began to sink. The prince was immediately put in a boat and pushed safely away, but he heard the stricken cries of one of his illegitimate sisters and went back to save her. Many other people then frantically climbed aboard as well, and the tiny lifeboat sank. Of the three hundred people aboard the *Blanche Nef*, two hundred ninety-nine drowned, including the prince. A butcher survived to tell the story of the tragedy.

No one had the courage to tell the king what had happened. He had to endure three days of agonizing suspense before the fainthearted barons sent a young page to tell him. Apparently the tragedy permanently soured his good disposition. He became so morose after the death of his only legitimate son that his council decided to force him to remarry as a last-ditch effort to cheer him up. They convinced him that he needed to beget a new heir, and accordingly, in 1121, he married Adelicia of Louvain, a pretty girl of about twenty. But ironically, the onetime playboy did not father any more children (though after his death Adelicia remarried and proved herself quite well able to bear children). By 1126 Henry realized it was hopeless, and he sent for the one remaining child of his first marriage, the totally unappealing Matilda (née Alice) and made the court swear to honor her as his heir.

One day in November, 1135, Henry went hunting and got tired and overheated. He finished off a meal of lampreys (primitive sea creatures superficially resembling eels), after which he suffered severe indigestion. Complications set in, and on December 1, 1135, he died at the age of sixty-seven. His passing marked the beginning of a bloody, devastating period in English history.

CHAPTER II

The Empress and the Angevins

Matilda
1102–1167

HENRY I's daughter Matilda was one of the most unappealing people in English history. She had been sent to Germany as a child bride of the Holy Roman Emperor, Henry V, but the aging monarch had died, leaving Matilda a childless widow. She was twenty-two when her father called her back to England to take her place as his heir. Matilda was a haughty, arrogant young woman who lived for politics and the glorification of her own ego, but she was her father's only hope of saving the Crown for his line. He forced the council, including his handsome amiable nephew, Stephen, to swear fealty to her as the next ruler of England. Henry I then got busy plotting her marriage to Geoffrey of Anjou, a young man who was in the habit of riding about with a sprig of greenery in his helmet called *planta genista* (Latin for a variety of broom, a shrub). It was from this that his descendants took the name "Plantagenet."

The greatest drawback to this marriage scheme was Matilda's impression of her own importance. Geoffrey was only fifteen years old and merely a count. Matilda was by then twenty-four and had been an empress. Henry had selected Geoffrey to lessen the possibility that Anjou, an important area bordering Normandy, might give Matilda trouble after her accession, but Matilda didn't see it that way. Besides, there were dark stories whispered about the counts of Anjou. They were said to be descendants of the Devil. One Angevin countess, forced into going to Mass, had disappeared under the very noses of her escorts and left only the strong smell of brimstone. Geoffrey never did anything that picturesque.

In spite of Matilda's injured dignity, Henry managed to get her married to Geoffrey in 1128. Matilda was not inclined to deprive anyone of her opinion, and she wasted little time letting Geoffrey in on what she thought of him. Naturally, Geoffrey wasn't crazy about her either, but he tolerated her for a year before sending her back to her father. Henry shot her back to Geoffrey. The stern-eyed young woman might be his daughter and heir, but that didn't mean he wanted her hanging around his court, criticizing his friends. Matilda bobbed back and forth between England and Anjou several times, growing more indignant and more unbearable each time. She finally managed to get busy producing a family, which curtailed her travels for a while. In 1133 she gave birth to a boy, who would become Henry II. Geoffrey was born in 1134 and William in 1136.

It was rumored during Henry II's lifetime that he was not Geoffrey's son. His birth followed a rather hasty return to Anjou on Matilda's part, and this trip had not been preceded by the months of bickering that usually occurred before Matilda's journeys. Considering the way that Matilda felt about Geoffrey, it's not altogether unbelievable that she was more attracted to her handsome cousin Stephen, who was always at court. Geoffrey apparently thought that was the case because he never made a move to help secure the crown for her or Henry and did all he could to leave his territories to his second son, whom he knew to be his own. It would certainly be one of history's greatest ironies if the proud and handsome kings who bore the name "Plantagenet" were not in fact related to Geoffrey of the *planta genista*.

While Matilda was in Anjou accumulating heirs, her father, Henry I, died. His nephew Stephen was with him at the end, and he wasted no time dashing to London to inform the population that Henry, from his deathbed, had repudiated Matilda and named him, Stephen, the rightful king. This was entirely false, but the people were willing to accept it for several reasons. First, Stephen was there and Matilda wasn't; second, Stephen was pleasant and easygoing and Matilda was obnoxious; and last— Stephen was a man.

Stephen, therefore, was set up as king of England and started preparing the way for his son, Eustace, to follow. Geoffrey's mismanagement of Anjou and his reluctance to get involved in Matilda's battles caused Matilda to waste nearly four years getting to England to claim what should have been her crown. She didn't have Geoffrey at her side when she finally got there. She had one of her many bastard brothers, Robert of Gloucester, who was a fine general.

This delay in getting to England was somewhat to Matilda's advantage because it gave Stephen ample time to prove to everyone how totally inept he was. Stephen wanted, most of all, to be liked; he had only the most remote idea of how to rule. In four years, he managed to lose most of his supporters, and it took Matilda only two years to scrape together enough followers to capture and imprison him. Flushed with victory, she strutted to London to take her place on the throne, but her manner was so completely offensive to the welcoming officials that she was run out of the city almost immediately. Soon after that, Stephen's wife (also named Matilda) managed to free him without Matilda's knowledge.

Eventually the barons who had swung over to Matilda's side got fed up with her arrogance and started scuttling back to Stephen's camp. Stephen's support grew, and he finally regained the crown.

For all the comic-opera overtones of this purely personal battle between two people equally unfit to rule, the effect on England was tragic. The barons, granted privileges from both sides in hope of their support, became minor tyrants in their own right. Their squabbles were fought by innocents, who either died of their wounds or starved. The laws were unenforced and the coinage was debased.

Matilda finally gave up the battle temporarily in 1147 when her half brother Robert died. Even she had sense enough to realize that without his military skill, she had no chance. She went back to Anjou to wait for her son Henry to grow up. Her husband Geoffrey, who had been dashing around capturing Norman castles during her absence, died a few years after her return.

By then, Henry was showing the leadership an authority he was to exercise throughout his notable reign. He landed in England in 1153 to take up where Matilda had left off. Stephen and England were tired and worn out and still licking the wounds of the long civil war. Rather than waste more lives, they came to an agreement. Stephen was to rule for the rest of his life and then the crown was to go to Henry. Stephen survived for only a year after that.

The fight seems to have gone out of Matilda. She came back to England briefly for her son's coronation and died in 1167 without any further foray into the politics of the country.

Henry II
1133–1189

HENRY II was one of the most dynamic personalities of his time. Twenty years of civil war had brought England to her knees. The country would probably have fallen into complete anarchy had not just such a brilliant administrator come to the throne. He was an overwhelmingly energetic man, who took a personal interest in every aspect of English life. No detail was small enough to escape his notice, or insignificant enough to be forgotten. His memory was phenomenal. Henry II had a devotion to justice and a concern for the welfare of his subjects that were not to be matched for many years. One of his greatest triumphs was bringing the overpowerful barons under his control. This was a massive accomplishment, for in the years of civil war preceding Henry's reign they had become "kings" in their own territories.

At the time Henry's ineffectual father, Geoffrey of Anjou, died, Henry was a short, thick youth of eighteen with curling reddish hair. He was not yet king of England, and he had to do homage to Louis VII, king of France, for Anjou. Henry had gone to Louis' court once before with Geoffrey and had already met the beautiful queen of

France, Eleanor of Aquitaine, but her situation had altered somewhat since that previous visit.

Eleanor had been the most sought after woman in Europe for most of her life. She was beautiful, intelligent, and rich. She also had an extremely healthy appetite for the opposite sex. Louis was a good man, in fact, a saintly man, so the marriage had been doomed from the start. Eleanor didn't especially care for a saint in her bed.

The division between them widened when Eleanor decided to go crusading with Louis, taking along a contingent of lady crusaders somewhat alarmingly attired in white tunics with red crosses and wearing high red boots. In spite of the ladies' baggage and squabbling, the crusaders finally reached Antioch. Once there Eleanor managed to excite lively rumors concerning her relationship with her handsome young uncle Raymond, ruler of Antioch. By the time Louis and Eleanor returned to France, it was clear to everyone that their marriage would have to be dissolved. They had two daughters but no male heirs whose legitimacy would be jeopardized by an annulment.

The wheels had been set in motion by the time Henry arrived at court. Henry and Eleanor must have been immediately attracted to each other's personal and political attributes, for things began to happen right away. In March of 1152, Eleanor's marriage to Louis was annulled. Six weeks later, Henry and Eleanor were married and an indecorous four months later, their first son was born.

Eleanor's wandering attentions were now permanently fixed on England and her family. Henry must have been quite a satisfactory husband for her, at least at first. He was a lusty, energetic man, which certainly couldn't be said of Louis.

At any rate, Eleanor's swinging style was cramped by

the fact that she was in her thirties now and had just given birth to the first of eight children she would bear Henry. The first son, William, was a frail child who died quite young. The second was Henry, who lived to be a young man but predeceased his father. The next son was Richard, who was to become Richard the Lionhearted. Another son, Geoffrey, died as a young man in a jousting accident, and the youngest son was to make his mark on history as King John. There were also three daughters: Matilda (English history of this period seems to be crawling with Matildas), Eleanor, and Joanna. The daughters all thrived and made good matches.

Henry and Eleanor were both fanatically devoted to their children, particularly their sons, but unfortunately each parent had a different favorite. Eleanor favored the handsome Richard. Henry was devoted to the unlovely John. This difference of opinion created great animosity between Henry and Eleanor and among their sons. The tragedy of their marriage was that these two incredibly intelligent, dynamic personalities wasted so much of their energy in what was little more than a family fight. The tragedy was increased by the fact that both of the favorites turned out to be miserably ineffective monarchs. Both Henry's spoiled sons turned against him early, joining together in various combinations with the cuckolded Louis' son Philip in an effort to displace him.*

Like many men of great mental capacities, Henry gave little thought to comfort, his own or anyone else's. His court was cold, mildewed, and dirty. Of course, by modern standards, the architecture and sanitation of the Middle

---

* Louis VII had remarried shortly after he and Eleanor parted company. Philip and his sister Alice were the result of Louis' second marriage.

Ages left a great deal to be desired under the best of circumstances, but Henry's surroundings were even worse than necessary. For one thing, there were very few ladies around—women, to be sure, but few ladies. By the time their sons started growing up, Henry and Eleanor were so much at each other's throats that he locked her up in a castle far from him for seventeen years, so the softening influence of a queen was not felt at court.

Henry went along with minimal concessions to his position. He wore valuable jewelry and clothing of expensive cloth, but he never had time for washing, changing, or fittings. A contemporary said that the only difference between the court and Hell was that you could hope to get away from court eventually. The nobles complained that it was necessary to drink Henry's wine with their teeth clamped shut to filter it.

Unfortunately Henry is often remembered primarily for his relationship with Thomas à Becket. Becket had come to Henry's attention early in his reign, and Henry was quick to realize that here was an intellect equal to his own, but different. Henry was roughhewn; Becket was refined. Henry could spot what had to be done in a given situation; Becket saw different ways of getting it accomplished. Henry was only one man; Becket was many, and when he took on a role, he took it on entirely.

Henry decided to make Becket archbishop of Canterbury as well as chancellor of England, thus making the Church more pliable. But he misjudged Becket. As Henry's friend, he had been a stimulating, witty conversationalist, with an empty place at his table always set for Henry. As Henry's chancellor, he was a talented, crafty politician, and Henry's interests were his own. As archbishop, however, he became single-mindedly religious. With great show he disposed of his riches, put on a hair shirt, and made the causes of the Church his causes. When Henry clashed with the Church, he found that he himself had put the most powerful enemy available at its head.

After years of dispute Becket was brutally murdered in his church by four knights who thought they were doing Henry a favor. Making a martyr of Becket was, of course, the last thing Henry wished and the one thing Becket had been seeking. It did great damage to Henry's reputation then and throughout history.

By this time Henry's struggles with his sons had begun. They were treacherous and ungrateful, but Henry made his full share of mistakes in dealing with them. It made an old man of him. Finally, tired and ill, he suffered a defeat at the hands of his son Richard and of Louis' son, Philip. The list of traitors was read to him, but he heard only the first name—John, his beloved son John. He said the rest didn't matter and turned away. He died a week later.

Richard I
1157–1199

RICHARD the Lionhearted was a handsome crusader, the flower of chivalry. He was little else. As a son, husband, and king he was a dismal failure. He became king at the age of thirty-two in 1189 upon the death of his father, Henry II. His first act was to free his mother, Eleanor of Aquitaine, who had been confined by Henry for the past seventeen years. Richard had lived most of his life in France. He now made the first of his two visits to England as king and began extracting every available asset that the country could give up in preparation for the Third Crusade. He wished to free Jerusalem from the Muslims.

This was not entirely a religious move or a political one; it was a military venture. Richard lived for war and combat, and a great Crusade promised more than the usual expectations of bloodshed and glory. England figured in his plans only in that he could draw upon its resources of men and supplies. He and King Philip of France, who was Richard's equal in treachery, made arrangements as uneasy allies for the Crusade.

Richard's advisers developed some brutally simple ways of raising the money to finance the venture. The first method involved several waves of crushing taxation. The second method was even simpler. Richard sold everything: appointments to Church and state offices, judicial decisions, castles, and lands. The buyers of the castles later found that they had to return them. Richard claimed that the money they had given him was a contribution. Bribery, so long as the profit went to Richard, became the law of the land.

Out of the crusading spirit grew some of the most shameful events of England's history. Anti-Semitism, always present in the Middle Ages, grew ferocious. The outward reason was that the Crusade was a Christian venture and that the Jews were considered enemies, albeit passive enemies, of the Church. The real reason was that the Jews, with their ingrained respect for business and finance, owned most of the money in England. Richard's coronation set off a series of tragedies for these unfortunate citizens.

Richard had issued a proclamation that no Jews or witches would be allowed to attend the coronation. The witches presumably stayed home, but a number of wealthy Jewish merchants felt that the expensive gifts they were bringing to the handsome, grasping young monarch would exempt them from the ruling. They were catastrophically mistaken. They were beaten severely, and some were killed. The Christians of York turned into a vicious mob that burned the area of the city where the Jews lived. A great many of the Jews took refuge in the palace at York, and when the mob started to burn them out, they cut their own throats rather than be captured.

Richard didn't officially approve of this bloodthirsty recreation, but he took advantage of it to make more money. He announced that the heir to all these unfortunate Jews was not their bereaved survivors but none other than the Crown. This included collecting all the debts owed the Jews by the Christians responsible for their deaths.

Richard had one other matter to settle before he started his Crusade. He needed to be married. He had one betrothed on hand. Alice, the sister of his sometime friend Philip, had been sent to Henry II's court as a child, and she grew up with Richard, her intended husband, which was a common practice. The flaw in the plan was that when she reached beddable age, she chose to be Henry's mistress rather than Richard's bride, and she remained so until Henry's death. All Europe knew about it.

Richard had no intention of marrying his father's hand-me-down. Instead, he married a shy, pretty, and not very important princess, Berengaria of Navarre. It's rather strange that he did so. She wasn't any political prize, and, for once, he didn't make any money on the deal.

Berengaria had seen Richard years before at a tournament and had fallen in love with him. Even though he was already betrothed at that time and was considered the best catch in Europe, she held out against all other proposals on the outside chance that Richard might someday want to marry her. Eventually her dreams were realized, or so it seemed. The sprightly old Eleanor of Aquitaine turned up in Navarre with a message from her son Richard. Berengaria was to get her things together in a hurry (no easy job for a princess in those days) , and Eleanor would take her to Marseilles, where Richard and Philip of France were organizing supplies and, incidentally, still arguing over what to do with Alice.

Berengaria did as she was bid and hurried to France. Richard and his ships had sailed, however, so the two women and their party traipsed across Europe trying to catch up with him. When they finally reached his camp at Cyprus, he took only enough notice of Berengaria to postpone the wedding.

Richard is said to have been homosexual, but if so, he didn't flaunt his preference. It may well be that in spite of his dazzlingly virile appearance, he just wasn't interested in sex—either of them. After all, sexual adventure, to a warrior, probably can't begin to compare with charging around slaughtering Muslims. It's hard to be intimate in armor. His relationship with the unfortunate love-struck Berengaria seems to bear this out. But for some reason of his own, Richard married her. He finally got around to sparing three days from his military activities for both a wedding and a honeymoon.

The Crusade was a failure, but through no fault of Richard—except perhaps an inability to get along with his allies. Not that they made any effort to be cooperative. They gave up and went home just as victory was within their grasp. Richard got within sight of the Holy City, but he couldn't capture it. He then refused to climb a small hill that afforded a view of the city, making what was possibly the only humble remark of his life. He said that if he couldn't *save* Jerusalem from the infidel, he had no right even to *look* upon it. Then he started back.

Eleanor had already gone back to England to keep an

eye on Richard's brother John, leaving Berengaria with Richard's sister Joanna, the widowed queen of Sicily.

Richard knew it was unsafe to travel openly through his former allies' countries, because an enormous bitterness among the European monarchs had been the chief result of the Crusade. So he sent Berengaria and his sister back to France and set off on his own. He thought they all had a better chance of getting home safely that way. It worked—for everybody except Richard. He was captured by the German emperor. The emperor sent word to John and Philip, who had joined forces in Richard's absence, that for an enormous ransom he would release the English king.

John and Philip sent back word that they would pay the ransom, if the emperor would promise to *keep* Richard instead, but Eleanor got wind of this plot, raised the money, and went to Germany with it to buy Richard back. The emperor sent a letter to John with the short, pointed message: "Look out. The Devil is loose."

Richard went back to England and repeated his coronation ceremony, presumably to remind John of the fact that he was still king. He did not invite Berengaria to join him in England. She was still waiting to meet him in France. In fact, Berengaria is unique among the queens of England in that she never set foot in England.

Richard didn't stay long in England either. He went back to France, where he got involved in a petty squabble over a small treasury of coins that had been found there. He and Philip both claimed the right to confiscate it. During the siege of Châlus that resulted, Richard got an arrow wound that became infected and gangrenous, and he died. He had been king of England for ten years and had spent about eleven months there.

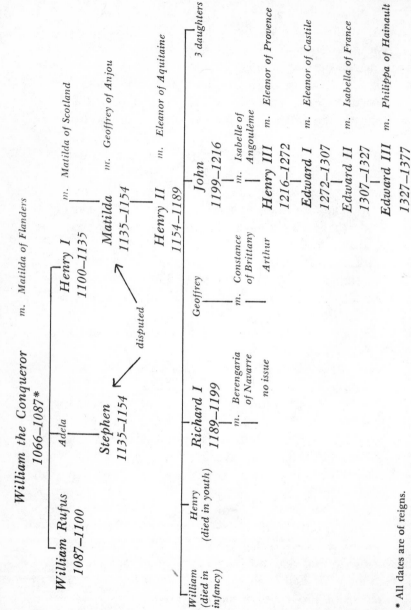

The English Succession
1066–1377

William the Conqueror
1066–1087*   m.   Matilda of Flanders

William Rufus   Adela   Henry I   m.   Matilda of Scotland
1087–1100   1100–1135

Henry   Stephen
(died in youth)   1135–1154   disputed   Matilda   m.   Geoffrey of Anjou
1135–1154

William   Richard I   m.   Berengaria   Geoffrey   m.   Constance   Henry II   m.   Eleanor of Aquitaine
(died in   1189–1199   of Navarre   of Brittany   1154–1189
infancy)   no issue   Arthur

John   m.   Isabelle of   3 daughters
1199–1216   Angoulême

Henry III   m.   Eleanor of Provence
1216–1272

Edward I   m.   Eleanor of Castile
1272–1307

Edward II   m.   Isabella of France
1307–1327

Edward III   m.   Philippa of Hainault
1327–1377

* All dates are of reigns.

John
1167–1216

THE untimely death of Richard I left the crown of England in the hands of his younger brother John. John, a short dark man lacking the hearty good looks of his family, was every bit as unprincipled as Richard, with the additional drawbacks that he was to reign somewhat longer and spend the time at home terrorizing his subjects.

Actually, to name John king, the line of succession had to be tampered with. There had been a brother born between Richard and John named Geoffrey. He had died as a young man only a few days before his wife gave birth to a son, Arthur of Brittany. Arthur should have been next in line, and Richard had even named him as his heir at one point, but he later changed his mind.

The barons of England heartily disliked and distrusted John, but they still preferred him to Arthur, who was only a boy of thirteen. Besides, John had grown up right under their noses, and they felt they knew what to expect from him. Arthur was a stranger who had never been in England. Moreover, his mother, Constance of Brittany, despised her husband's family, and Arthur was reputed to be just as grasping and deceitful as John, and it seemed possible that he would grow up to be even worse.

John was in England when word of Richard's death reached him. He immediately claimed the crown. The barons probably gave a shudder and crossed themselves in private, but no one objected publicly except Arthur and his mother Constance.

John had inherited England and about two thirds of what is now France. Early in his reign he set out on a tour of his French possessions, and one of his stops was at Angoulême. Count Aymer of Angoulême had no sons.

His heir was his daughter Isabelle, who was something of a medieval Lolita. She was only twelve or thirteen when they met, but John, who was an experienced lecher, was completely overwhelmed. A marriage to her would have been politically useful except for two things: John was already married, and Isabelle was betrothed.

Then, as now, most of Europe's royal houses were related through years of intermarriage. The Church had an elaborate system of rules of consanguinity, forbidding marriage within certain degrees of kinship. The rules could be circumvented by papal dispensations, and the dispensations could then be reversed or nullified if necessary, so that while there was theoretically no such thing as divorce, in practice it was fairly common, or at least possible, among the upper classes. John had married a distant cousin, Isabella of Gloucester, without a papal dispensation, so it was easy for him to get the marriage annulled. Isabella, after ten years of marriage to him, was entirely agreeable.

The closest modern equivalent to a betrothal is an engagement, but they aren't quite the same. Unlike a modern engagement, a betrothal was not a social contract between individuals but a binding legal agreement between two families. Isabelle, like many highborn young women, was sent as a child to be raised by the family of her intended husband, Hugh de Lusignan. Of course, breaking their betrothal in order to marry John was an enormous insult to Hugh de Lusignan, who was anxious to marry Isabelle now that she was of age. Hugh didn't do anything then (there wasn't much he could do), but he set out to ally himself with John's greatest enemies, Arthur of Brittany and King Philip of France. Hugh would meet John later, as would Arthur. Meanwhile, John and Isabelle, after a hasty marriage, returned to England and John set about making more enemies for himself.

Were it not for his cruelty, John's faults and excesses might be almost forgivable. He was an intellectual and a skeptic at a time when such characteristics were virtually unknown. He could be a clear-headed organizer when he felt it was worth the trouble. He had a cynical sense of humor, which would probably be appreciated more today than it was then. Pretentiousness and formality often inspired him to such improprieties as pulling beards, blowing kisses, and winking at pompous officials. He was at thirty-three a somewhat unattractive man with a carefully tended beard and thick, sensual features. He believed in complete self-indulgence in matters of clothes, food, drink, jewelry, and women. In an age when a castle started waking and stirring long before dawn, John disgusted the court with his slothful habit of staying in bed with his pretty child wife until noon. He had no regard for any principle or for any individual except his mother, Eleanor of Aquitaine. Whatever provided immediate self-gratification was his policy. Many people in lesser positions have shared these characteristics; what history has been unable to overlook is John's cruelty.

During the first years of John's reign his nephew Arthur had been at King Philip's court collecting support for his claim to John's throne. He had accumulated a good-sized army, so John was finally obliged to get out of bed and cross the Channel to protect his French possessions.

Largely by accident, Arthur managed to stumble into his grandmother, Eleanor of Aquitaine, at a town called Mirabeau, and he called in Hugh de Lusignan, who was busy stirring up trouble nearby. Eleanor took refuge in the castle at Mirabeau and sent a plea to John for help.

It was a desperate situation for Eleanor, but Arthur in his contempt for her had misjudged his grandmother. She was eighty years old, which was a phenomenal age in those days, but Eleanor had always been a remarkable woman. She didn't give up as an old lady would be expected to, but took command of her band of followers to resist Arthur's siege. In the meantime John, for once in his life, moved so fast that he amazed everyone. He and his troops covered the eighty miles to Mirabeau in forty-eight hours and took Arthur and Hugh completely by surprise. John had captured them and their knights before they had time to realize he was there.

This one worthwhile act of John's life was tarnished by what followed. The captured knights were taken to England. With the exception of Arthur and Hugh, they were all locked up and starved to death. Hugh was eventually released, presumably at Isabelle's request.

Arthur was also locked up but he was never seen again. John certainly had him killed; the mystery is how. The most widespread story was that John got drunk and disagreeable one night, killed Arthur with his own hand, and dumped the body in the river. Another version was that Arthur died of shock and blood loss as a result of being blinded and castrated. Whichever (if either) was true, it is a measure of John's reputation for cruelty that both versions were widely circulated and given credence.

It was at about this time that Eleanor died. John's enemies invented a pretty story of her dying of a broken heart because of John's treatment of Arthur, but that was an absurdity. Eleanor knew John far too well to have been shocked at anything he might do. Besides, she hated Arthur as much as John did. She died because she was well over eighty years old in an era when people were usually gray and toothless at forty.

Arthur's death is the background of the other and possibly blackest mark against John's name. A crony of John, William de Broase, had been in charge of keeping Arthur imprisoned. After Arthur's disappearance de Broase became so much wealthier and more powerful that it was obvious he had some hold over John. Finally de Broase got a little too greedy, and he and John had a falling out. John demanded that de Broase send his son to court as a page, a euphemism meaning as a hostage to ensure compliance. This was John's standard policy. De Broase's wife Maud had a notoriously outspoken manner and she refused to send the child, making an ill-advised statement that she wouldn't turn her son over to a man who had murdered his own nephew.

One can imagine the stunned silence that must have followed *that* remark, from the one woman in England who had reason to know Arthur's fate. Maud realized that she had gone one step too far and tried to retract the statement, but it was clear that she had sealed her family's fate. They tried to escape, but John caught up with Maud and the child. She and her son were locked up together, and John's favorite method of death, starvation, was employed again. It was difficult enough to accept the death of knights (who knew they were risking their lives by opposing a monarch) by this method, but the death of a mother and her child by such a cruel, slow means was unthinkable. This act did even more than anything else to damage John's already shaky reputation with the barons of England.

The next problem John was to encounter was the Church. England was a distant outpost of Christendom, and religious life there had a flavor all its own. The Church as an organization, however, was a rich and powerful political entity, powerful enough to chafe many kings.

This struggle between the power of the Church and the power of the state had been the basis of Henry II's feud with Becket.

John's troubles with the Church came about over the same office, archbishop of Canterbury. John and Pope Innocent III each had a favorite candidate, and the Pope saw to it that his choice got the post. John made various threats about what would happen if the new archbishop set foot in England, but Innocent was not to be bullied. He excommunicated John and laid an interdict on all of England, which deprived everyone of the functions of the Church. Birth, death, and coupling went on but without the Christian sacraments. The plight of the common people was dreadful. The sacraments were mysterious, powerful, and comforting. Without them, life was grim, and death—no confession, no absolution—might presage damnation. Even ordinary days had always been punctuated and ordered by the bells of the village church, and the people felt lost without these familiar sounds. Interdict lasted for five years, from 1208 to 1213, when the Pope started making dark remarks about John's French possessions. John gave in.

The catalog of John's infamous acts would be incomplete without one story concerning his domestic life. John had married Isabelle in 1200 and years later was still jealously infatuated with her. Characteristically, his infatuation didn't preclude a generous sampling of other charms. Of course, this didn't work both ways, and when he suspected that Isabelle wasn't practicing absolute fidelity (he was probably right), he had the suspected gentleman hanged over her bed. In spite of this incident, they remained on intimate terms, and Isabelle, by then about twenty years old, gave birth in 1207 to the boy who would become Henry III. The next child was Richard, and three daughters followed. The oldest daughter was betrothed as an infant to, of *all* people, Hugh de Lusignan, to whom Isabelle had originally been betrothed.

It is nearly impossible to speak of King John without the words "Magna Carta" echoing in the background. John and his brother Richard had been tyrants in their own ways, but John was the more offensive. It was largely his abuse of power that led the barons to join forces and draw up a list of rules he had to follow.

The Magna Carta was a landmark in that it asserted that the nobility, the knights, the merchants and craftsmen of the towns, and the freemen had certain rights that the king couldn't tamper with, and that the king had a responsibility for the welfare of the country. It was not a statement of political philosophy but was simply a list of specific rules for specific situations such as inheritance, forest use, and standardized measurements, and it attempted to check abuses in the administration of justice. Its importance, however, lay not in its contents but in the fact that it existed at all and that a feudal group could force their master to seal it.

And in view of the united front of all his barons, John did give in and signed the Magna Carta at a meadow called Runnymede in June of 1215. Then, after a series of spectacular tantrums, he repudiated the entire thing. By that time the sense of cooperation among the barons was beginning to fray, and civil war ensued. It didn't last long, however, due to John's death in October 1216. Chilled and fatigued by his travels, during which he carted around nearly every movable possession he valued, including jewels, money, gold plate, and his grandmother Matilda's crown, he had ordered his wagons to cross a stream only a short distance from where it emptied into the sea. As the tide suddenly came in, John watched helplessly as men, wagons, horses, and his treasures were suddenly swallowed up by water and quicksand. None of it was ever recovered.

Cold, wet, and discouraged, he went to a nearby monastery, where he finished off a meal with cider and peaches and became quite ill. He insisted on moving that night to Newark in spite of pain and fever, and died there of dysentery, leaving a completely disordered country to his nine-year-old son, King Henry III.

Unlike many dowager queens who quietly fade away, Isabelle led quite a busy life after John's death. She broke Hugh de Lusignan's betrothal to her small daughter and married him herself. Poor Hugh had waited many years for her and lived to regret it. She first produced a good-sized family for him and then proceeded to nag him into all sorts of fights with the French over slights both real and imaginary. When an attempt was made in 1245 to poison the king of France, Isabelle was implicated. She fled to a monastery and died there a year later. Hugh and her sons emerged from the episode alive but stripped of all honor and most of their lands. Considering John's appreciation of the absurd and his contempt for Hugh, he probably would have been delighted at the outcome of his wife's second marriage.

Henry III
1207–1272

HENRY III is remembered for encouraging architecture and for having a drooping eyelid, because that is the best that can be said about him. He came to the

throne as a nine-year-old boy, and his intellectual develop-
ment seems to have dried up at that point. He was the
son of the archvillain, King John, and father of the remarkable Edward I. Henry never adhered to any one
course of action long enough to qualify as a good king or
a bad king.

Henry became king in 1216. The title meant little, as
he was a child and the country was in a state of civil up-
heaval over his father's abusive politics. The young king
and his country were entrusted to a group of counselors,
who were of two camps. One group was the English
barons, led by Hubert de Burgh. The other group, the
"foreigners," was headed by Peter des Roches, a young
bishop whose main interest was to bring as much wealth
to himself and the Church as England could provide. Des
Roches and his supporters mainly came from England's
French possessions and had been appointed to important
positions by King John. They had a condescending contempt for anything English.

In spite of personal differences, it was agreed that everyone's best interest would be served if they settled the
civil war, which had also become a war with France when
John's disgruntled barons had offered the crown to Prince
Louis, heir to the French throne. Now John was gone, but
the king of France still demanded the crown. The argument was finally settled in an exciting battle in the
English Channel in which Hubert de Burgh played a
courageous role and became a hero to the people. England
settled down to relative peace under his direction. Henry
liked him, as well he might, for Hubert was making an
efficient business of replenishing the depleted treasury,
mainly at the expense of the barons.

In 1227, at the age of nineteen, Henry announced that

he was assuming full responsibilities. This was a vast over-statement. He decided that a war would be a glamorous way to begin his reign, and the next year he found an excuse to go fight with France. Hubert de Burgh objected. So did everyone else with any sense, but it was de Burgh's objection that Henry remembered. The campaign was a complete failure. Henry's troops were either defeated or ignored everywhere they went. It didn't take Henry long to fix on de Burgh as a scapegoat.

Henry's accomplice in his extended harassment of de Burgh was Peter des Roches. The crafty bishop had already been in and out of Henry's cyclic affections several times. In 1231 he swooped back to court as Henry's best friend.

De Burgh realized that he was cornered, with des Roches pouring his opinions into Henry's vacant head. He took sanctuary in a church and was dragged out and taken to the Tower of London, but Henry and his henchman became uneasy about having violated sanctuary. After all, ruining an enemy was acceptable, but certain rules had to be followed. Therefore, with typical medieval reasoning, they decided to take de Burgh back to the church. Then his tormentors settled down to wait for him to give up voluntarily. They didn't let any food go in, so it didn't take long for de Burgh to come out. With superstition satisfied, they again imprisoned him.

When de Burgh learned that he was to be turned over to Peter des Roches, his long-time enemy, he contrived to escape and make another mad dash for a nearby church. The whole silly routine of sanctuary, violation-of-sanctuary, and restoration-to-sanctuary was repeated, but this time de Burgh managed to get away before hunger got the best of him. He fled the country.

A few years later Henry swung back from his violent hatred of de Burgh and allowed him to return to England. Relations between them remained cordial until de Burgh's daughter impulsively married a man whom Henry had planned to marry off elsewhere. Henry then trotted out all the old accusations against de Burgh. He didn't get much support this time, because everyone knew better than to think any judgment of Henry would be permanent. Before anything could be done, the tired old man's beloved daughter, who had brought about the whole flare-up, died, and Henry lost interest in the renewed persecution of the man who had held his kingdom in trust for him while he was growing up. Hubert de Burgh was allowed to crawl away, and he died quietly some years later.

During this time Henry had been under the spell of Peter des Roches, who had been calmly and efficiently confiscating every penny and every acre he could and stashing it away with friends and relatives. He was so critical of the English nobility and so grasping that the barons finally descended on Henry with proof of des Roches' treachery that even Henry couldn't overlook. Henry did another characteristic about-face. His full fury now fell on this bishop who had been making such a fool of him. Des Roches fled the country. He was gone for several years, and when he returned, Henry again welcomed him with open arms. Fortunately des Roches was too ill and tired by then to attempt to regain his former power, because Henry would almost certainly have tried to restore it to him.

Life at court must have been a seesaw nightmare for those who were obliged to maintain Henry's favor, but they might have been warned early in his reign by his treatment of his mother. Isabelle of Angoulême had left England shortly after King John's death. In 1220 she had married the man to whom she had been betrothed as a girl. She sent a message announcing the marriage to her son, and he not only cut off her income but wrote to the Pope demanding that his mother and her new husband be excommunicated. The Pope replied, diplomatically but clearly, that Isabelle's marriage was her own business, not Henry's. Of course, Henry was only thirteen years old at the time and was parroting what his advisers told him, but it was an age when boys of thirteen sometimes led armies, and he could have asserted himself on his mother's behalf if he had wished.

The only person Henry remained true to was his wife. He had suffered years of rejections by eligible princesses when his attention fell on Eleanor of Provence. Her family was cultured, fecund, and very poor, although they never let that interfere with their inclination for luxurious living. Henry was determined to have her, and in 1236 the twenty-nine-year-old bachelor and the fourteen-year-old beauty were married.

Eleanor brought along an army of freeloading relatives who refused to go home after the festivities. Henry was completely infatuated with his wife, and since she had a keen sense of kinship it wasn't long before her uncles, brothers, and cousins started infesting every vacant post in England. The barons were alarmed at this influx of offensive foreigners, and they blamed Eleanor because they were her relatives and because it was her influence over her witless spouse that was causing all the discontent.

In spite of their unpopularity with everyone else, Henry and Eleanor were an unusually happy royal couple. There was never any hint of scandal about either of them. Their first child, born in 1239, was to grow up to be the handsome blond giant known as Edward I, or Edward Longshanks. Another son and three daughters completed the exceptionally close family. Henry's sons were far more clever than he was, but through all his antics they remained completely loyal to him. In view of the number of royal sons in history who have itched to depose their fathers, Edward I showed admirable restraint.

Henry III also had a sister of whom he was very fond. She fell in love with an intelligent young man by the name of Simon de Montfort. They were secretly married in 1238 with Henry as their only witness and with his full approval. De Montfort rose in favor for about two years. Then, with a typical change of heart, Henry found some pretense for getting angry and publicly insulted the couple, bleating about how Simon de Montfort had seduced the king's sister. He had them turned out of their lodgings, and they very sensibly left England immediately.

It didn't take Henry long to forget the whole episode and decide to "forgive" them. However, Simon de Montfort was a man of integrity whose memory was not so short nor his pride so flexible as to let him forget the crude, groundless accusation. He did manage to be reasonably polite to Henry, and for his efforts he was put in charge of Gascony, one of England's remaining toeholds in Aquitaine. With great trouble and personal expense de Montfort managed to get Gascony under control in less than half of the seven years that had been allotted for the job. He returned triumphant to resign his post and be reimbursed for the expenses he had incurred in England's behalf.

Henry's tenuous grasp on the concept of justice then became completely unglued. He demanded that de Montfort be brought to trial and forced to continue to finance the administration of Gascony personally for the remainder of the seven years. During all this Henry was more insulting and offensive than ever, but in spite of his shrill invectives the judges cleared de Montfort of all charges and ordered Henry to repay the expenses in question.

Henry went off in a huff to settle Gascony's affairs himself, leaving Eleanor in charge at home. She immediately got busy inventing special taxes for London. It created very bad feelings, and she was later to regret having recklessly offended the people of that city.

While Henry was on that trip he arranged the marriage of his son Edward, by then a gigantic teen-ager, to Eleanor of Castile, a lovely young girl who was to be loved by the English as thoroughly as her mother-in-law was hated.

When Henry returned, it was to face a crisis in his reign. His wife's family had been a trial to the barons for years. Henry had also allowed his mother's good-for-nothing sons by her second marriage to strut around making pampered nuisances of themselves. Shortly after Henry's return, it came out that he had put England enormously into debt in a half-baked private deal with the Pope to buy the crown of Sicily for his second son. The barons would have no part of it, and what is more, they decided that Henry could no longer be allowed full powers. They drew up a list of provisions in 1258 providing a check on Henry's authority, which Henry sullenly agreed to.

But Henry had a breezy disregard for keeping his word. He sent secret messengers to the Pope, who was anxious to support Henry's position, mainly because Henry owed the Pope money. In 1261 a papal bull was issued, absolving Henry from the oath he had taken to observe the provision. Civil war was inevitable.

Most of the barons who opposed Henry simply wanted to ensure their own welfare, but they realized that what was good for England was also good for them, and Henry definitely wasn't good for anyone. They weren't trying to overthrow him, just leash him. They wanted to get some control over him before he plunged the country into some irreparable disaster. England had been wobbling along on the brinks of various catastrophes ever since Henry had come of age thirty-four years before.

Simon de Montfort was naturally at the head of the opposition. A fast-paced civil war ensued, and the barons were victorious. One memorable feature of the whole episode was Queen Eleanor's attempted escape. She tried to sail out of London in the royal barge, but when she reached London Bridge, she was greeted by a barrage of rocks, mud, and rotten vegetables. She retreated. The English have neglected some queens, beheaded a few, and laughed at many, but never have they exhibited such vituperative hatred as they did toward Eleanor.

Henry remained a tamed king for a year, with de Montfort running things, an arrangement that might have lasted longer if it hadn't been for Prince Edward. De Montfort had confined Prince Edward at Hereford Castle. In 1265 he escaped and led a crushing revolt against de Montfort's forces. Henry's long-time enemy was defeated, killed, and mutilated.

Henry regained his authority, but in spite of this, calm prevailed for the remaining seven years of his life. Edward spent the first five of those years running things for Henry, partly because he was better qualified, and partly because Henry was deeply involved in the completion of his lifelong dream: St. Edward's chapel at Westminster.

Henry died in November of 1272 and was buried in the newly completed chapel. He had been king of England for fifty-six years and had led a long and foolish life.

CHAPTER **III**

The Royal Sandwich

Edward I
1239–1307

EDWARD I, Edward II, and Edward III form a personality sandwich. Two of them were warrior-heroes who had long lives. The man between was a shallow fool who died young and unmourned.

Edward I had a brush with greatness; unfortunately, he didn't recognize it, and it passed him by. As a young king he had the idea that the baronage wasn't the only important class of English society, that the common people had certain contributions to make and some rights as well. In the context of feudal society it verged on heresy to suggest that anyone who was not of nobility or knighthood actually had a say in politics—that is, in how a nation was governed.

Edward summoned the first Parliament that consisted of two houses: Lords and Commons. Edward's Commons didn't have much to say—in fact, they were in Parliament chiefly to vote the king money—but they were there. Edward either lost interest or lost faith in these ideals as he aged, but his youthful idealism had set in motion political forces that would have a profound effect on the course of Western civilization.

63

Edward was six feet two, which was a towering height in the Middle Ages. He had the handsome Plantagenet features and reddish-blond coloring. Fortunately, he shared few of the qualities of his butterfly father, Henry III, except a deep devotion to his family. He was married at the age of fifteen in 1254 to the ten-year-old Eleanor of Castile. Shortly thereafter he was drawn into a civil muddle of his father's making and saw little of her for several years. When at last he had settled England's affairs and returned to her, he discovered that his child bride had become a beautiful woman. He fell very much in love with his wife, and she was entirely devoted to him. Two sons and a daughter were born in quick succession. In 1270 Edward and his prolific wife left England and the children to go on a Crusade. As they were returning two years later, Edward received word that his oldest son and his father had died and that he was now king. Shortly after the news reached them, Eleanor gave birth to another son.

Eleanor's childbearing record seems extraordinary. She gave birth to her first child when she was twenty-one, and she continued, until her death at age forty-seven, to produce children (mainly girls) with amazing regularity. It is quite certain that she had four sons (the records of the day kept close track of sons), but only one survived childhood. She had eleven daughters whose names are known. Several other daughters were born but didn't live long enough to be named. Some of the daughters died young, and only one lived to middle age.*

----

* Though the number of children born to them and their high mortality rate is surprising to us, it was not exceptional for the times. The average family had five to ten children, a great many of whom were stillborn, while many others died of childhood diseases.

Edward didn't hurry back to England when he heard of his father's death. In fact, he spent almost two years in Europe, socializing with fellow monarchs and settling odds and ends of business in his continental possessions. When he finally did reach England, he plunged into the job of ruling with an energy that was unabated for the rest of his long reign. He didn't always rule with wisdom, but he always exhibited the philosophy that kingship was a responsibility, not a privilege. He believed strongly in his divine right to rule, for he felt that he had good evidence for such belief. Before he became king, he had twice missed death by inches in freak accidents. On one occasion lightning killed two people standing behind him. The other incident involved a large stone, which fell from the ceiling onto his chair only seconds after he had impulsively moved away.

Edward's first military excursion upon his accession was against Wales. The English and their Welsh neighbors had been on chronically bad terms for as long as anyone could remember, and subduing them was a prodigious task. The Welsh were wildly independent and of volcanic temperament. The average Welsh chieftain could match a Plantagenet rage any day. After Edward defeated them and then held court in Wales, he had to revive an old rule that it was a punishable offense to hit the queen or to wrench objects out of her hands, for the Welsh thought nothing of hitting a queen.

While the royal family was in Wales in 1284, Eleanor gave birth to the boy who was to be Edward II. Caernarvon Castle was not entirely completed then, but Eleanor did have a tiny (eight by twelve feet) unheated room high in the tower. The baby's cradle still exists. The castle itself has not fared so well, although it was in adequate repair for the courtyard to be the site of the investiture of Prince Charles as prince of Wales in the summer of 1969.

Edward's most serious mistake was in thinking that, once he had some semblance of control over Wales, he could do the same with Scotland. There were major differences between them that Edward either didn't realize or wouldn't acknowledge. Scotland wasn't as close to the hub of England as Wales, and Edward was getting old and cranky.

In 1290 the direct heir to the Scottish throne died, leaving such a multitude of contenders for the crown that in desperation the Scots called on Edward to mediate the dispute. Edward was seduced into thinking that this was an acknowledgment of his overlordship and gave him the right to interfere in Scotland's affairs. The Scots thought not. Edward fabricated some flimsy excuses for invading Scotland and attacked the town of Berwick. The citizens gathered on the walls of the fortifications and sang derogatory ditties to "Edward Longshanks," a designation that drove Edward over the walls in a black fury. Once the town was taken, Edward ordered all the male citizens put to death. This sort of mass execution was inexcusable, and Edward finally relented, but by then many thousands of people had already been slaughtered. It's difficult to see why Edward found "Longshanks" insulting; he wasn't especially long-legged, just very tall.

The slaughter at Berwick was not only a moral error, it was a tactical mistake. It fired up the Scots with a zeal previously unknown and brought forth William Wallace, a legendary warrior who was to outwit Edward's troops and become a national hero. Edward spent the rest of his life fighting the Scots, but he never managed to defeat their independent spirit.

It was in 1290, near the beginning of his problem with Scotland, that Edward lost his beloved Eleanor. She had been traveling with him, but stayed behind at one point because she wasn't feeling well. Within days Edward got news that she was much worse. She was dying. Edward flew to her side, but he was too late.

The king was disconsolate at the death of his gentle consort. He took Eleanor's body back to Westminster for the funeral. It was a slow journey, with crowds of mourners joining along the way. The journey took almost two weeks, and Edward later had English artisans build a beautiful monument at the site of each night's stop. These were the famous Eleanor Crosses.

Eleanor's effigy shows a pretty woman, not of faddish beauty but with timelessly lovely features. Her death was a great blow to Edward, and almost three years passed before another marriage was arranged. It is easy to suspect him of disloyalty to Eleanor's memory, but more was involved than Edward's feelings. Of his enormous brood of children fewer than half were still living, and of his sons, only one remained. Edward was an astute statesman. He might have suspected that this son was fated to be a personal and political failure and that it might be wise to have another heir to the throne lined up.

Edward's choice for his second wife was Blanche, a sister of the king of France, but Blanche was very beautiful and very conceited, and a crusty old campaigner wasn't her idea of romance. She had her younger sister's name substituted for hers in the treaty (royal marriages always involved treaties, which were seldom honored), and six years elapsed while Edward and King Philip haggled over the sisters and all the other complaints that existed between the two great powers. Finally, in 1299, Edward and the younger sister, Marguerite, were married. He was sixty-two, she was twenty. The treaty involved in their marriage provided that Edward's son would marry Philip's granddaughter, who was Marguerite's niece. This union was to be one of the most tragically destructive in English history.

Marguerite was much like Eleanor in personality—kind, gentle, and devoted—although not so pretty. She was greatly admired for her generosity and even temper. Edward had only seven years to live, and in that time Marguerite provided him with two sons and a daughter (named for his first wife, Eleanor).

Edward didn't have much time to spend with Marguerite at first, because he was so busy fighting with Scotland. She soon realized that the solution was to adopt Eleanor's policy of going along. She was with him on an expedition to Scotland in July of 1307 when he died. Although he had retained his teeth and sharp vision, he was almost seventy years old and had been ill for nearly a year. Marguerite was still in her twenties, but she lived only ten years more, and she never remarried or even considered it. Apparently she had truly loved the leathery old warrior.

It is regrettable that Edward tarnished his name with the long futile fight with Scotland. Had he maintained his policies of peace and justice that characterized his middle years, he would shine through history as an even brighter light in the Middle Ages than he does.

Edward II
1284–1327

EDWARD II was a homosexual. In his case it was a terminal affliction, fatal to him and to his favorites. In all aspects of kingship—dignity, power, responsibility—he was the Plantagenets' most spectacular failure. He was willing to give up anything for his own pleasure, and in inevitable succession he forfeited his power, his wife, his son, his throne, and his life.

Edward was a sole surviving son among a great flock of sisters. His timid mother had died when he was only six, and during his youth his aging warrior father had kept him on a short leash. He was forced to follow his father about, accepting a great deal of unwanted advice and even more criticism. These facts may account, in part, for his later actions, but nothing could possibly excuse them.

Edward II formed a friendship with an acquisitive young knight named Piers Gaveston while they were both in their teens. Edward's father sent Gaveston out of the country when he discovered the depth of their relationship. It was not only the sexual aspect (which must have been repugnant to a man like Edward I) that disturbed him. Gaveston's quick wit ran largely to elaborate and cruel practical jokes, gambling, and drinking. Prince Edward was not particularly bright. He was extremely impressionable and completely infatuated with Piers.

Obviously the old king's precautions had come too late, for Edward II's first act as king was to recall Piers. His next move was to get married, which seemed out of character except that there were several reasons for the marriage that made sense even to Edward. The primary consideration was that the girl was wealthy and Piers was greedy. The bride, Isabella of France, was a girl of thirteen. Edward was twenty-three, so he found it easy to consider her a child rather than a woman to interfere with his devotion to Piers. The betrothal had been arranged years before between Edward and Isabella, who was the daughter of King Philip the Handsome and Joan, queen of Navarre. Isabella's Aunt Marguerite was Edward's young stepmother.

Edward went to France to marry Isabella, leaving Piers as regent. This was a blow to Thomas of Lancaster, who as Edward's first cousin and nearest adult male relative should have been named regent. (Thomas was the son of Edward I's younger brother, Edmund Crouchback.) Edward's reckless choice was obviously meant to be irritating.

The wedding was celebrated in France with great pomp, and Edward behaved himself until his return with his bride. Then he bounded off the ship and went flying into Piers's arms, leaving Isabella to perform her own introductions. To top it off, Piers turned up the next day wearing several items of the expensive jewelry that Isabella's father had given Edward as a wedding gift.

Isabella made an immediate hit with the English. She was an extraordinarily pretty girl (although certainly not the sexless child Edward thought her to be), and she made an effort to be charming to everyone. More important, the English sympathized with her—she was married to a fool for their sake. However, her function was to beget heirs, and that was going to be tricky with a husband who didn't understand whose bed he belonged in.

Edward put Piers in charge of the coronation ceremony. Piers wasn't capable of organizing a family picnic, much less a coronation, and it turned out to be a disaster. Everything was late, there weren't enough seats for everyone, the service for the dinner was nearly nonexistent, and the food was variously stale, raw, burned, and meager. Piers sauntered through the whole thing dressed so magnificently that the king looked like a country cousin. But Edward was dewy-eyed with adoration for his clever Piers.

Had it not been the ultimate breach of etiquette, the barons would have poisoned Piers on the spot.

The barons got together and forced Edward to send Piers away, but the separation lasted only a year. When he came back, everyone tried to ignore him in the hope that either Edward's infatuation or Piers's vanity might have diminished. They were disappointed on both counts. At a tournament held shortly after Piers's return, he amused himself by out-jousting everyone and bestowing very personal and cutting nicknames on the barons. He had a gift for finding everyone's sorest spot and probing it unmercifully. For example, one knight had an embarrassing habit of involuntarily spitting when he talked. Piers named him "mad dog" and called him that at every opportunity.

The barons despised Piers for himself, not for his relationship to Edward. They wouldn't have cared what the unlikely lovers did in private if Piers had stayed out of their way. However, Edward not only allowed Piers to offend the barons but encouraged, in fact, delighted in it. The difficulty is to determine just where pity ends and contempt begins in dealing with these two. Between them they didn't have an ounce of self-preservation. It is astonishing that Edward never reflected on the problems that his grandfather, Henry III, and his great-grandfather, King John, had suffered by offending their barons.

The pressure against Piers increased until Edward even agreed to turn over his authority as king to a council of barons called the Ordainers just so long as they left Piers alone. It would have been more sensible for him to urge Piers to curb his vicious tongue than to give up his power, but common sense wasn't Edward's long suit. The Ordainers immediately threw Piers out, but in defiance of them he came right back. Edward's cousin Lancaster had been treasuring up grudges since the regency incident, so he and his supporters went after Piers in force. Piers fled, and Edward fled with him. They even dragged Isabella along, although they dumped her along the way because she was slowing them down—she was pregnant and getting bulky. How she managed to catch Edward's attention long enough to get pregnant is a mystery.

Piers and Edward got separated, and Piers was captured. Sadly for him, he had in his possession part of the crown jewels and a quantity of gold and silver belonging to the court. It's hard to see how a pregnant queen could have been much of an added burden to someone carting all that around. A small group of barons secretly took Piers out to an isolated hill in the middle of the night of June 13, 1312, and beheaded him without a trial. Although it's difficult to discern any good in Piers, there is one thing to his credit. He was loyal to Edward; his lacerating wit was never turned on his king. Instead of the bickering that is common to such couples, they were always in accord, each trusting the other.

Edward was mad with grief at the news of Piers's death. In all fairness to him, he loved Piers with a intensity that is rare in any relationship. Had he kept Piers out of the spotlight and conducted himself with a minimum of dignity and responsibility, they might have had a pleasant life together.

Piers's death gained Edward some sympathy. Many of the barons felt that not giving him a trial had looked bad, although a death verdict would have been certain. More likely, they were simply miffed at having been excluded from the beheading party. Now that Piers was out of the way, there was more to be gained from being friendly to the pliable king rather than his overbearing cousin Lancaster, who had been at the head of the opposition.

On November 13, 1312, Isabella gave birth to a son, who was named for his father and his grandfather. For the only time in the reign of Edward II, everyone was happy. Piers's death had left a great emotional hole in Edward's life, but a healthy baby can absorb much fatherly affection. Isabella was pleased, for finally her place was ensured. With a male heir there was no possibility of an annulment, so she no longer had to make very much effort to get along with her husband. It seems they did get along, however, as there was another son born to them in 1314, and then two daughters.

Edward had not been cured of his poor judgment, only temporarily distracted. Through all his previous troubles, only one baron had stuck by him. Hugh Despenser was a Marcher baron*, and he had a good-looking son about Edward's age (young Hugh), whom he kept at court. Despenser felt that Edward would eventually become enamored of young Hugh, and, of course, the crafty old man was right. The situation with Piers was repeated, and Edward became a willing pawn of the Despensers. But they were a worse threat than Piers Gaveston. They wanted more than money, they wanted power, and they were far too smart to offend people deliberately. The barons couldn't pin down any specific complaint, so while the Despensers pandered to Edward at court, the barons raided, robbed, and burned a good part of the enormous Despenser holdings. They finally forced Edward to exile the hated family.

---

* The Marches was a large area bordering Wales. Important families were granted huge tracts of land there and great power in return for which they kept a constant guard on the borders. These wealthy, powerful, and generally arrogant lords were the Marcher barons. Traditionally, they had less respect for, and less to fear from, the king than any other barons.

The Despensers were gone by the time of the battle of
Leeds Castle in 1321. Isabella had been traveling and
had sent word ahead to Leeds Castle that she and her
party would spend the night there. It was Isabella's property, but the woman whose husband held it for her decided for some insane reason of her own not to let the
queen in. When they arrived, this virago had her archers
shoot into the group, killing several of Isabella's company
and narrowly missing the queen. Isabella was justifiably
furious, and for once in their marriage, Edward was on
her side. He gathered his troops and stormed the castle. It
was the only military victory of his reign. He became a
minor hero and, hence, had a lever to regain some power.
But rather than do himself some good, the poor fool used
the lever to recall the Despensers.

At this time Lancaster and Roger Mortimer, another
warlike Marcher baron, started up a rebellion in the
Marches. Edward arrived, ready to fight, but Lancaster
neglected to show up, leaving Mortimer holding the bag.
Mortimer ended up in the Tower.

Mortimer was probably the most ruthlessly ambitious
man of his time. He also happened to be extremely attractive. His stay in the Tower coincided with Isabella's
(she wasn't locked up, just staying in the royal apart-
ments). To put a beautiful, lusty and frustrated woman
in the same building with a sexy man who happens to be
her homosexual husband's worst enemy will produce an
inevitable result. Isabella now embarked on a course that
was to reveal her as just as blindly and foolishly passionate
as Edward at his worst.

Mortimer made a bold escape from the Tower in 1323.
As escape from the Tower was nearly impossible, he obviously must have had help in high places. The only per-

son who had any interest in his welfare was Isabella, so it is assumed that she was a party to his plan. He went directly to the French court, where Isabella's brother Charles was king. Isabella went to France in 1324, supposedly to negotiate some matters of state, actually to join Mortimer. She stayed until 1325, and then requested that Prince Edward join her there to do homage for England's French possessions on Edward's behalf. Edward stupidly allowed the boy to go but then found that he couldn't get either the queen or the prince to come back. The prince was only thirteen years old, so he didn't have much to say in the matter with Mortimer running the show.

Isabella sent word that they would return as soon as Edward sent the Despensers away, but even though it meant getting his wife and son back, Edward wouldn't part with them. He just went on writing letters to the tune of "I can't see why everybody's so mad at *me*." By 1326, Isabella's prolonged visit with her brother was becoming an embarrassment to him. She and Mortimer made no secret of their affair, and Charles was tired of all those whining letters from his brother-in-law. His suggestions that she move along got less and less polite. Finally, the queen, her son, and her lover moved in on Isabella's Flemish cousin and her husband, the count of Hainault, who had four sturdy daughters, one of whom was destined to be the next queen of England.

Isabella had to return to England for the sake of her son's inheritance, but she couldn't go back unless she could get control over Edward. She gathered an army and returned in 1326. Edward didn't even attempt to organize an opposing force. He and the Despensers simply scattered. The elder Despenser was caught, tried for treason in Isabella's presence, and hanged immediately. Edward and

Hugh were apprehended trying to get out of England. Hugh refused to eat once he was captured and had nearly succeeded in starving himself to death when Isabella had him killed. Parliament met in December to depose of Edward II and crown his son.

Edward wasn't treated too badly at first, but his jailers became progressively more antagonistic. Obviously Edward couldn't be allowed to live. Politics ruled that a deposed monarch had to die soon afterward. Otherwise, he would act as an automatic magnet to anyone who became dissatisfied with the usurper. It was hoped that by subjecting him to dismal and filthy living conditions he would obligingly die of a "natural cause," such as dysentery or pneumonia, but a year after his capture he was miserable but still quite healthy.

On the night of September 22, 1327, Edward was pinned down on a table, and his jailers killed him by thrusting hot irons into his abdomen through a funnel in his rectum. Theoretically, this sadism was conducted so that there would be no external marks of violence, but his agonized screams, which roused the town of Berkeley, and the expression of suffering on his dead face gave the lie to this theory. (Or so the story goes.) His face was said to be so horribly distorted as to be almost unrecognizable, which gave his sympathizers the opportunity to claim that the real Edward had escaped and that the body was a substitution. Isabella and Mortimer made very short work of anyone who tried to spread such rumors.

Mortimer certainly gave the order for Edward's death, and Isabella must have known that her husband was to be killed, but it isn't clear whether she knew when or how. By this time, she had appropriated most of the crown revenues for herself and Mortimer, and had let him usurp all her son's authority. After the news of Edward II's death was made known, the people began referring to her as the "she-wolf of France." Her fate and Mortimer's belong to the story of Edward III.

Edward III
1312–1377

EDWARD III was fourteen when his mother and her lover had his father killed. He was only a puppet king, and certainly had no knowledge of the plans Isabella and Mortimer had for his father. In fact, they didn't even bother to consult with him about any of their schemes. He was forced to treat Mortimer as respectfully as if the overbearing baron himself were king, and for the first few years of his reign, he could do nothing to oppose him. His mother was completely enthralled with Mortimer, who had already murdered one king and wouldn't hesitate to murder another one. Edward was smart enough to detach himself from them in the public's eye whenever possible. Every time they made any display of their greedy activities, he managed to be too busy elsewhere to take part. Thus he managed to keep from sharing their unpopularity. They didn't seem to notice.

Isabella and Mortimer sent Edward off to fight a pointless war in Scotland to keep him out of their way. No one could have beaten the Scots with the small force he had, certainly not an unskilled boy. Young kings learned about war from their fathers and older generals, and since his father had never been at all interested in military affairs, Edward had a serious disadvantage. He lost the war, but took advantage of the experience to learn a great deal about where he went wrong. He was to make war his life's work.

He came back to find that his wife-to-be had arrived in England. Philippa of Hainaut's suitability was one thing that Edward and his mother agreed on. Philippa was one of the four daughters of Isabella's Flemish cousin. She was a plump, pretty girl of fourteen when she and Edward were married in January of 1328. They stayed as far from Isabella's court as possible.

Isabella and Mortimer seriously misjudged Edward. They thought his apparent disinterest indicated dumb pliability; actually, he was coolly observing, weighing, choosing, and waiting for the right opportunity to take things in his own hands.

In June, 1330, Philippa gave birth to a son who was named Edward, and who would be remembered as the Black Prince. Apparently, this event made Edward feel that it was time to assert himself. On October 19, 1330, Edward, Isabella, and Mortimer were staying at Nottingham Castle. The place was locked up like a safe, because Isabella was beginning to sense that they had enemies, but Edward had found out that there was an ancient, unused tunnel leading from the outside to the heart of the castle. A group of young men, handpicked by Edward for their loyalty to him, sneaked in, stormed Mortimer's room, and seized him. They killed the men who were with Mortimer.

The noise awakened Isabella in the adjoining room. She dashed in and pleaded passionately with Edward to spare "gentle Mortimer." No one else was the least inclined to plead his cause. He was taken to the Tower of London where he was tried and condemned without being given any chance to defend himself. He was hanged, drawn, and quartered.

Edward was very careful not to allow Mortimer any chance to implicate Isabella. There were a number of reasons for this, one of which was filial devotion, though that must have been strained by this time. As a proud new father he must have been particularly disgusted with his unfaithful mother. In addition, there was a practical, political reason for keeping Isabella's name out of the proceedings.

It had become almost a tradition since William the Conqueror for the French and English monarchs to make periodic snatches at one another's crowns, and Edward, a bright young man, saw his opportunity coming up. Isabella's father, Philip the Handsome, had been king of France. There had been a curse put on the family which, as curses go, had been pretty effective. Philip had died shortly after incurring it, leaving three sons. They each had a short turn at the throne, and each had died without male issue. The next of kin left was Isabella, their sister, but French law prohibited a woman on the throne. Understandably, Edward didn't want the crown to go *to* her but thought it ought to pass *through* her to him. Except that French law expressly forbade it, it wasn't a bad claim. Naturally, had Isabella's reputation become officially besmirched by a trial for treason, it would have been hard on Edward's claim. Nevertheless, the crown went to Isabella's uncle.

Isabella was sent to Castle Rising, a dull, remote place. Rumor had it that she suffered spells of madness after Mortimer's death. She must have been at least a little crazy to endure the years of monotony at her grim, lonely fortress. Edward paid duty calls on her once or twice a year for the rest of her life. She lived there quietly until her death twenty-seven years later. She had an adequate household and got to travel occasionally.

Now Edward was king in fact, not just in title, and his character became clearer. He was in adult life a continuation of his warrior grandfather. They were of the same cut, but Edward III had more frills. Edward III continued Edward I's campaign for control over Scotland and took on France besides. He was the handsomest of a beautiful family. His effigy shows a long stern face, a straight nose, a flowing beard, and piercing eyes. He and his plump little Flemish wife must have been an attractive pair, especially as Edward believed in spending lavishly on clothing and jewels.

Edward settled down to raising a family and trying to get enough money for a fight with France. In January, 1340, he made his first official move to begin what historians would label the Hundred Years' War. He added the lilies, symbol of France, to his banner. The first battle was on sea, and Edward enjoyed the victory. Unfortunately, it gained him nothing but prestige. Not an acre changed hands, and a truce was declared.

Philippa was waiting in Ghent, and on June 24, 1340, the day after the battle, she gave birth to her fourth son, John of Ghent, or, as he came to be called, John of Gaunt. (One son had died in infancy.)

Everyone went home to borrow the money to resume the war. Edward's life was a long story of money problems. He liked his court to be showy, and that was enormously expensive when you realize that "court" included hundreds of people, all salaried. The royal family all had personal attendants who required the services of tailors, laundresses, cooks, bookkeepers, furniture makers, and so forth. The buildings and grounds had to be maintained, so did the horses and livestock. Edward never had the faintest idea of how to economize. He went so far into debt that he bankrupted two international banking firms.

Edward III had all the characteristics that make a showy and memorable king, but few that make for real greatness. He was a good military man and lived for the romantic but impractical ideas of chivalry. In1348 he set up the Order of the Garter to honor knighthood and preserve the fading concept of chivalric deeds, but he did little for the common soldier.

English literature and commerce flourished during Edward's reign, but they did so in spite of royal indifference. The humdrum business of taxes, laws, courts and such domestic business rather bored him. Still, he maintained the peace within his realm that allowed these things to exist and grow.

The second important battle with France was in Crécy in 1346. Edward's oldest son was now sixteen years old and wearing the black armor from which came the appellation "the Black Prince." Edward and the Black Prince were the victors through a combination of skill, geography, and good luck. French knighthood was nearly wiped out.

At the same time, there were a few sailors dying mysteriously in ports on the Black Sea. Edward didn't know about them and wouldn't have been much interested if he had known, but within two years their deaths would be profoundly important to him, because they had died of the plague. The disease slithered across Europe and reached England in 1348. Without preventatives or even an understanding of how the contagion spread, it had the same effect on human life as a forest fire has on trees. Entire families died; life took on a mad, end-of-the-world morality. Nearly half the population of England was dead when it abated.

Only one of those deaths was really important to Edward and Philippa. Their thirteen-year-old daughter Joanna was on her way to her marriage in Spain when the ugly disease caught and killed her within hours. Her parents were heartbroken. They were very close to all of their children, especially this daughter born to them in their youth.

It is characteristic of Edward that while the Black Death was carrying off half his subjects, he was making weighty decisions regarding the garments and ceremony for his Knights of the Garter. Nothing could keep him and his oldest son from war for long. In September, 1356, the battle of Poitiers was fought. The Black Prince was in charge and not only won the battle but brought back two important trophies, the king of France and his son. They were entertained royally for months while the underlings haggled over ransoms and exchanged hostages. At one point, the king of France was even allowed to go home to help raise the money for his own ransom, and failing to, he returned to England, voluntarily! Such was the triumph of chivalry over common sense.

Edward's heroic reputation became blurred in his old age, as he became senile. Philippa began to suffer from dropsy in 1367, and the silly old man took one of her ladies (a misnomer in this case), Alice Perrers, as his mistress. When Philippa died in 1369, Edward turned over her jewelry and personal possessions to Alice.

Alice interfered with the government to such an extent that Parliament officially criticized her and ordered Edward to keep her out of state business. The old fighter had degenerated to the point that he meekly accepted the rebuke and tried to do as he was told.

In 1376, a slow cancer finally claimed the Black Prince,

at the age of forty-six. He left a nine-year-old son, Richard, as Edward's heir. The death of his oldest son was the final blow for the senile old man. He deteriorated rapidly and died in 1377. Alice Perrers was with him at the end and stayed until nearly everyone who had been present at his death had left the room. Then she took the rings off his dead fingers and left.

This king, who had showed such promise at his accession, had started the Hundred Year's War and had fathered the families of the Wars of the Roses.

CHAPTER **IV**

The Wars of the Roses
Overview

THE Wars of the Roses were an extended domestic
bloodbath that went on for many years and destroyed many
families. The wars wiped out the Plantagenets and deci-
mated the nobility. During those years there were seven
Plantagenet kings, four of whom were deposed and killed.
Any discussion of the tangle of cousins involved always
returns to four of the sons of Edward III who survived
infancy. Even though none of them were directly involved,
their descendants were, so it is necessary to pause here and
sort them out.

The oldest son was Edward, the Black Prince. He had
appeared to be a tenacious bachelor until a plump little
widow called Joan of Kent managed to extract a proposal
from him. She presented him with two sons, one of whom
survived. The Black Prince died a year before his father,
leaving his nine-year-old son as heir to the throne. This
child was named Richard, and as King Richard II, he
set the wheels in motion for the Wars of the Roses.

Edward III's second son was Lionel, a good-hearted giant
of a man. He had only one child, a daughter, who married
into the Mortimer family (the same Mortimers who

figured in the overthrow of Edward II). Thus, her child, a Mortimer, was next in line for the throne after Richard. The throne never came to Lionel but his descendants were the Yorks, who were to oust Henry VI under the banner of the white rose.

To further complicate things Edward III's next son, John of Gaunt, the duke of Lancaster, was married three times and had two entire families involved. He is an interesting figure in English history because nearly everything he did is open to contradictory interpretation. A few things are certain: he was sophisticated, intellectual, and very rich. Financially, he controlled more of England than the king.

John married Blanche of Lancaster, an heiress, and fathered the boy who would be Henry IV and represent the red rose. Blanche died young, and John took as his mistress Katherine Swynford (who was, incidentally, Geoffrey Chaucer's sister-in-law). She bore him three sons, who were given the family name Beaufort. John married again, but when his second duchess died, he astounded the court by marrying Katherine. He then petitioned his nephew Richard, who was now king, to have his grown Beaufort children legitimatized. Richard agreed to the plan. The oldest Beaufort son eventually had a granddaughter, Margaret, who married Edmund Tudor. They were the parents of Henry VII. A Beaufort daughter married a Neville and was an ancestress of the York branch of the family.

Edward III's fifth son was Edmund of Langley, the duke of York. His son married into Lionel's family and was the grandfather of Edward IV.

Edward III had a sixth son, Thomas of Woodstock. He was an insensitive lout who gave Richard II a great deal of trouble, but fortunately for the family genealogy he didn't have descendants involved in the wars.

Roughly speaking, then, the crown bounced from the family of Edward the Black Prince to John of Gaunt's legitimate family (the Lancasters), to the descendants of Lionel and Edmund (the Yorks), and finally back to John of Gaunt's illegitimate line (the Tudors).

"If-only-ing" is a fruitless historical exercise, but it can be a fascinating and irresistible game. This particular period lends itself well to that sort of speculation. The Wars of the Roses would have been avoided or curtailed . . .

If Richard II had not inherited the throne at such an early age.

If Richard had not succumbed through greed or pride to the temptation to seize the Lancaster wealth.

If Lionel had not married.

If Henry V had not married the daughter of a madman.

If the English had adopted the Salic Law, which prevented the right to the succession from passing through a female line. (Of course, in this case they would have had to forgo such fortunate reigns as those of Elizabeth I, Victoria, and Anne.)

A legend, dramatized by Shakespeare in Part I, Act II, of his "historical" play *Henry VI,* has adherents of the two sides meeting in a rose garden, where they fall to quarreling over the claims of the rival houses. Thereupon, to show which side they are on, Lancastrian followers pluck and pin on themselves red roses and Yorkists white—from which incident comes the name "Wars of the Roses."

In actual fact, the term was invented by the Tudors

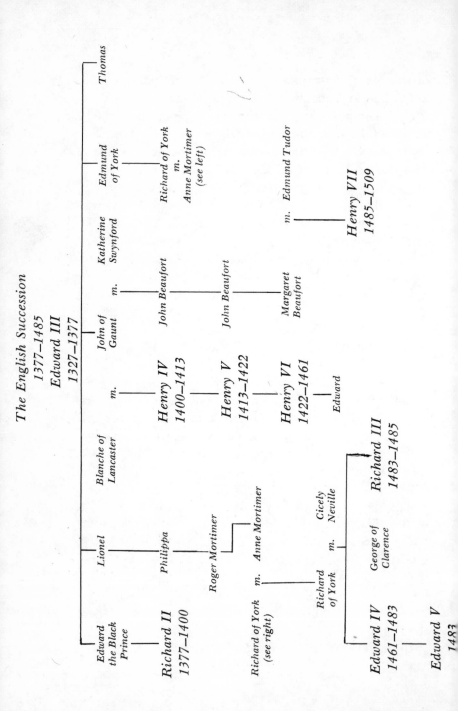

The English Succession
1377–1485

Edward III
1327–1377

Edward the Black Prince — Lionel — John of Gaunt — Edmund of York — Thomas

Richard II
1377–1400

Philippa

John of Gaunt
m. Blanche of Lancaster — Henry IV 1400–1413
m. Katherine Swynford — John Beaufort

Roger Mortimer

Henry IV
1400–1413 — Henry V 1413–1422

John Beaufort

Edmund of York
Richard of York
m. Anne Mortimer
(see left)

Richard of York
(see right)
m. Anne Mortimer

Henry V
1413–1422 — Henry VI 1422–1461

Margaret Beaufort
m. Edmund Tudor

Richard of York
m. Cicely Neville

Henry VI
1422–1461 — Edward

Henry VII
1485–1509

Edward IV
1461–1483

George of Clarence

Richard III
1483–1485

Edward V
1483

in the following century. The white rose was the family badge of the York family, although once they had come to the throne, they preferred the sun-in-splendor device, a sun with irregular rays emanating from it. (Sometimes the two were combined and became the *rose-en-soleil* or rose-in-splendor.) The Lancaster family had many different badges, the most common being an ostrich feather. Henry IV, a confused man, displayed at various times as many as twelve devices, one of which was a red rose. However, when Henry Tudor seized the crown in 1485, he wanted to propagandize himself as the bringer of peace between warring factions, so he created a badge that displayed a white and a red rose intertwined and called it the Tudor rose.

Nevertheless historians found the term "Wars of the Roses" so useful and colorful that they have continued to use it to this day. So will we.

Richard II
1367–1400

RICHARD II was out of touch with the times. He was too cultured, too peace-loving, too sensitive to hold a medieval throne. His was a stormy reign, full of changes and surprises. Quite often he did the right thing, but invariably he did it too soon or too late. Richard is credited with inventing the handkerchief or, as the household accounts called it, "little pieces of cloth for the king to cleanse his nose," and as trivial as it sounds, the handkerchief was symptomatic of the orgy of culture and art that marked his reign. He was vitally interested in and knowledgeable about all phases of sophisticated life: poetry, music, art, architecture. Even fashion and cooking were of importance to the sensitive, intellectual (and consequently doomed) young man.

He came to the throne as a ten-year-old boy, and a council was appointed to make decisions for him until he came of age. During the reign of Richard's grandfather, Edward III, the plague had swept through Europe, and the loss of between one third and one half of the population had upset the labor force. With fewer workers available, the ones left should have been able to insist on better wages. Instead, legislation was passed forbidding the serfs to seek better pay elsewhere. They were considered the property of the landholder.

Prices went up, church dues kept going up, and to this Edward III had added taxes to support his wars with France. Finally, in the summer of 1381, in the fourth year of Richard's reign, the boiling point was reached. Thousands of peasants marched on London, burning and looting along the way. They demanded to see the king. They had the naive belief that this pretty child really had the power to change their lives.

Richard, with the ego and bravado that often go with being fourteen, seemed to believe it too, and it was an opportunity to be in the limelight. He agreed to meet the leaders of the revolt at Mile End, a field outside London, and at that meeting agreed to grant their demands. The next morning there was another meeting. One of the rebel leaders, Wat Tyler, became so offensive and disrespectful that several members of Richard's group lost their heads and killed him on the spot. Richard immediately rode into the seething mob at great risk to himself and asked why the people needed Wat Tyler when they had King Richard on their side.

This courageous move was successful, and the mob went home, but Parliament and the royal uncles were not so easily swayed. They negated all the concessions Richard had made, and nobody gained from the episode. Richard's first great move had come too soon. He was still too young and inexperienced to use the upswing in his popularity to crowd out his elders and take control of the country.

Richard didn't seem the type to take control from these hard-bitten medieval barons. They had very little in common with him. Richard was handsome in a pretty, delicate way, and he was fastidious, which was a term that couldn't be used to describe the average nobleman. He thrived on music, art, fashion, and reading. Above all, he thought peace was preferable to war, and this last was inexcusable. As far as the nobility were concerned, England's constant striving to annihilate France, and vice versa, was all that kept the world going.

Richard was a high-strung, sensitive boy who would probably have behaved very foolishly during his years of constraint had it not been for a superb marital arrangement. The winter after the Peasant Revolt, he married Anne of Bohemia, a girl of his age who shared his interests, but who was wrapped in a thick layer of placid common sense. Anne understood Richard as well as anyone ever would, and she sympathized with and encouraged him. By her example, he learned to control his temper and practice patience.

Chief among those determined to keep Richard in check was his surly youngest uncle, Thomas of Woodstock, duke of Gloucester. During the first years of Richard's reign, Thomas became progressively more and more domineering. He kept nibbling at Richard's small fund of authority until Richard was virtually his prisoner. At one point, Thomas and his supporters demanded of Richard that he either endorse their policies or be deposed.

One of Thomas's supporters was Henry of Bolingbroke, John of Gaunt's son. As the eldest surving son of Edward III, John of Gaunt would have had a valid claim to rule instead of Richard, but he respected his father's wish to see Richard on the throne. John's son Henry had no such scruples.

Richard's second great moment came in a council meeting in 1389. After years of harassment by Thomas of Woodstock, Richard simply announced that he was of age and would henceforth rule by himself. He threw out Thomas and his friends and issued a proclamation to the country. By this skillful use of the element of surprise, he actually managed to get control. The one fatal flaw in the plan was that he didn't destroy his enemies immediately. Not only did they retain their heads, they were allowed to retain important posts, and eventually they wormed their way back into the council.

Once Richard got the opportunity to rule, he ruled well for a while. He indicated a real concern for the commoners. It is impossible to determine whether he was simply soft-hearted and felt sorry for them in their miserable conditions or whether he had the wisdom to recognize that a country's greatness rests in the well-being of all its people. Either way, he did what he could for them, although, strangely, he wasn't as well liked as when he had been an ineffectual child.

Richard's decline began with the death of his wife Anne, in June of 1394, because she had been not only an adoring wife, but an astute adviser and good friend. Richard became engulfed in his own feelings. He ordered that the castle where she died be torn down, and when one of his old enemies made a point of prancing in late to the funeral, Richard wordlessly grabbed a ceremonial wand and smacked him on the head so hard that the man fell down and bled all over the church floor. Anne would have deplored such violent, unprincely behavior.

The one thing Richard needed most Anne hadn't given him, an heir to the throne, so there was great pressure on him to remarry. After all, the continuation of the line is the first duty of a king. Two years after Anne's death, he married Isabella of Valois, the seven-year-old daughter of the king of France. He chose her because the marriage would help make peace with France and because it would be years before he would have to play the role of husband. This was both selfish and unwise of Richard. The more unstable his position became, the more he needed a son. Perhaps it was just as well, though. Isabella's father was quite insane, and later when her sister married Henry V, she brought the trait into the Plantagenet family.

Not until late in 1397 did Richard belatedly begin to long for revenge against his enemies. He had the earl of Arundel (the one who came late to Anne's funeral) arrested and put to death. Uncle Thomas was also arrested, and he died shortly afterward under suspicious circumstances. This left Richard's cousin, Henry of Bolingbroke, still to be dealt with.

Unfortunately Richard had acted too late. He couldn't dredge up Henry's traitorous behavior from ten years before with any hope of successfully getting rid of him, because in the interval, Henry had been playing the part of a loyal subject. Richard saw some hope in a quarrel between Henry and a young nobleman named Thomas de Mowbray. Henry came to Richard with the story that

Mowbray had uttered treasonable remarks to him. Mowbray denied it and declared Henry the traitor. There was
no way to determine what had actually passed between
them, so Richard allowed them to make plans for a fight
to the death in a tournament. Apparently Richard felt
that by letting them mutilate one another in public he
would be rid of one or the other of them, possibly even
both. He had good cause to believe either of them perfectly capable of treachery, given the chance, but when
the day arrived and the combatants were mounted and
ready to charge, he changed his mind. He called the fight
off and exiled both of them, Mowbray for life and Henry
for ten years.

The decision was quite silly and pointless. Nothing is
quite so dangerous as an enemy who is left free to hatch
plots just outside the victim's jurisdiction.

Richard was showing signs of degenerating mentally.
He talked constantly, and after years of having no power
he was now demanding ultimate power. But the days of
William the Conqueror were gone; a king would never
again be the entire law of England. Richard was just too
much involved in his own vindictive emotional jag to
realize it. He was a sensitive neurotic who had gone over
the brink; he was beyond making any sensible judgments.

In February of 1399, John of Gaunt died, making the
exiled Henry duke of Lancaster and the richest man in (or
in this case "out of") England. Richard then made his
greatest mistake. He declared the vast Lancaster inheritance forfeit to the crown.

To do Henry justice, no one could have let that go by.
The barons were frightened. If Richard was allowed to
do that to Henry, his own first cousin, imagine what he
could do to lesser men. Richard compounded his error

by going off to Ireland to settle some long-stale dispute there. It is useless to try to guess his reasons for this action. By that time Richard was functioning not by motivation but rather by impulse. He was being foolish and illogical, and he was flirting with the disaster that was shortly to overcome him.

By July of 1399, Henry had landed in England full of righteous indignation only to find that the king had gone to Ireland. Henry began by saying that he merely wanted his own lands back. Of course, he wanted the crown too, but he was hard pressed to come up with any valid-sounding excuse for claiming a right to it. The next in line to Richard was an eight-year-old boy, a descendant of Lionel's daughter.

By the time Richard realized what was happening and dashed back, he was again too late. His armies evaporated when the extent of Henry's support became known.

Richard gave in to Henry voluntarily. In September of the same year, Richard II went before Parliament and read his abdication. Henry then claimed the throne with a vague reference to being the grandson of Edward III (so were a great many other people). Richard was kept at Pontefract Castle for four months until it became obvious Henry already had enemies and couldn't afford to have a rightful king about. Clearly, Richard had to die, and as with Edward II, he showed no signs of doing so without help. He was thirty-three years old and in perfect health.

But he did die, on February 14, 1400, and certainly by violence. His body was then brought to London with great pomp. Only his face could be seen. His head was sunk in a deep, black pillow, and the rest of him was completely concealed. Henry's men tried to foster a rumor that

Richard had starved himself to death. They were not widely believed.

A life style died with Richard II. His dream of peace in England was not to be realized except in brief snatches for another hundred years. After his death the flourishing of arts declined. It is ironic that one of England's greatest writers, Geoffrey Chaucer, born in the same year as the cultured John of Gaunt, died in the same year as Richard II.

CHAPTER V

The Roses-Red

Henry IV
1366–1413

HENRY IV was one of those unfortunate people who get the one thing they want in life, only to find that they are stuck with an intolerable burden. Born only seven months after his cousin Richard II, Henry found his life shadowed by Richard, especially after Richard's death.

Henry of Bolingbroke was the oldest son of John of Gaunt, the duke of Lancaster, and his first wife, Blanche. He was born in 1367 and grew up in the company of a regiment of royal cousins, which included Richard. Henry and Richard probably never hit it off very well, because they were very different. In his youth, Henry was a hot-headed warrior, uncomfortable away from his horses and weapons, very much like Richard's father, the Black Prince. Richard, with his intellectual, artistic bent, resembled Henry's sophisticated father.

As a young man, Henry married Mary de Bohun, who was then barely past childhood. Mary and her older sister Eleanor were a case of Beauty and the Beast. The older sister was tactless, greedy, and unattractive. To compound her flaws she was married to Thomas of Woodstock, the youngest of Edward III's sons, whose capacity for getting along with other human beings was negligible. But Thomas found the disagreeable Eleanor attractive because she and Mary were the richest heiresses in England.

Thomas and his ugly wife had decided that half the Bohun fortune was a nice thing to have but that *all* the Bohun fortune would be even nicer. Therefore they had begun speaking to Mary of the benefits of the spiritual life. Mary was a kindly, devout girl who might have become a nun as they wished had she not met Henry of Bolingbroke. Mary and Henry fell very much in love, and were considered to be the ideal couple, except, of course, by Thomas and Eleanor.

The marriage of Mary and Henry was happy but short. They were married in 1384, when the groom was eighteen and the bride thirteen. Three years later, at Monmouth Castle, their first child, Henry, was born. Seven years and six children later Mary died. She was only twenty-three. It was to be many years before Henry remarried.

During most of his cousin Richard's reign, Henry of Bolingbroke could never quite determine what line to take. He was part of the overbearing council that bullied and threatened the young king, but later he started taking Richard's side. For years he behaved loyally, at least on the surface, but though Richard was impractical and slightly unbalanced, he wasn't stupid, at least not when it came to assessing Henry. Richard finally exiled his two-faced cousin.

Henry went to Paris to brood over the situation and wait out the period of exile, but in 1399 Richard made his fatal mistake. When Henry's father died in February, Richard not only seized the enormous Lancaster inheritance but extended Henry's ten-year exile to life. As Richard also had Henry's sons in England, this left Henry with just exactly nothing—no lands, no money, no country, and no family. Pride and self-preservation demanded that he put up some kind of fight.

Within a few months Henry landed in England, armed to the teeth and claiming that he only wanted his inheritance back. It must have been somewhat anticlimactic when Richard submitted to him without a nice bloody battle. Nevertheless, Henry now had what he wanted— the chance to be king.

The crown wasn't rightfully Henry's, because Richard was still living. Henry wasn't even next in line. That position was held by a boy who was a descendant of Lionel, an older brother of Henry's father. Henry must have convinced himself that he would make a better king than the neurotic or the child—and he was probably right —but that wasn't sufficient justification to seize a throne, so in the end Henry and Parliament decided to dispense with justifications and get on with the coronation. When Richard, in the prime of life and good health, suddenly died, everyone naturally assumed that Henry was responsible and didn't let it trouble them much. But it troubled Henry.

A great many things were beginning to trouble Henry. Besides an uneasy conscience he had a ruinous financial problem. Rebellions, even bloodless ones, are devastatingly expensive, and the Parliament that had put Henry IV on the throne didn't propose to pay his bills for the usurpation. His creditors, notably the Percys (Shakespeare's Hotspur and his father), weren't outstandingly charitable about not being repaid for their help. They therefore raised their own rebellion, which Henry managed to put down, but again at great moral and monetary cost. This was only one of the many rebellions with which he had to contend.

The only bright spot in his reign (and it's stretching a

point to call her that) was his second wife. Joanna of Navarre had been the third wife* of John de Montfort, duke of Brittany. Shortly after Henry (whom she had met several times) became king, Joanna's husband died, and she was left a thirty-two-year-old widow with nine children. She immediately set about getting a papal dispensation to remarry, but with a blank on the dispensation for the groom's name. She sent her representative, a man by the name of Antoine, to Henry with the news of the dispensation and her availability, and Henry agreed to marry her. Presumably there had been some previous discreet agreement between them.

It appeared, however, that Joanna wasn't too sure of herself. She didn't want to give Henry an opportunity to think too long or too deeply about the prospect and possibly change his mind. She couldn't leave Brittany herself until a great deal of business resulting from her husband's death had been cleared up, so she empowered Antoine to serve as her proxy as well as her messenger. For that reason, on April 3, 1402, the court assembled to watch Henry in wedding finery place a delicate gold band on a large hairy finger and solemnly intone to Antoine, "I, Henry, take thee, Joanna . . ."

With Henry legally committed to her, Joanna set Brittany's affairs straight and arrived in England the following February, having been officially married to Henry for ten months. She brought only the two youngest of her nine children along. Joanna was considered greedy and dull

---

* Just as an example of the tangled relationships that existed between royal families, Joanna was a great-granddaughter of Louis X of France. Her husband's first wife was Mary Plantagenet, daughter of Edward III. His second wife was Jane Holland, a half sister of Richard II. This example is not given because it is unique but because it is typical.

and wasn't especially well liked, but she didn't seem to care. She took good care of Henry during the last ten years of his life and always took his side. That alone made her unusual. Henry's son was later to lock her up for four years on charges of witchcraft.

By 1405, Henry was only thirty-eight years old, but the healthy young warrior who had seized his cousin's crown had grown old and bent under its weight. He had become a bitter, cranky hypochondriac. He suffered a severe skin rash, which everyone was glad to believe was leprosy, although it almost certainly wasn't. He suffered fainting attacks, which verged on comas; his heart began to fail, and he became suspicious of everyone, especially his son, Henry of Monmouth later Henry V, who was running things for him when he was ill.

By 1411, his condition was so poor that his advisers suggested he abdicate in favor of his son. He was outraged at the idea, and held his son, now known as Prince Hal, to blame. There was an ugly scene between them, and Henry managed to live another two years, surviving, it seemed, on pure nastiness.

He had been told that he would die in Jerusalem and felt quite secure that he would live till he made the pilgrimage. But in March of 1413, he became ill during a church service and was taken to the abbot's chamber to recuperate. Noting the religious tapestries, he asked the name of the room. The answer? . . . Jerusalem. He finally gave up and died, a disappointed, elderly man of forty-six.

Henry V
1387–1422

WHEN Henry V came to the throne at the age of twenty-six, he had already lived a full—if precocious—life.

He was seven when his mother died, which, since his father was abroad during most of his youth, made him effectually an orphan. At ten he was the guest of King Richard on the latter's trip to Ireland—part hostage for his father's behavior and part protégé with a generous allowance. Some time in the middle of the Irish campaign, Richard knighted the boy, then perhaps eleven years old.

At twelve, the year of Henry IV's accession, he was summoned home by the father he scarcely knew and created prince of Wales. Since the principality that gave him his title was in a state of armed rebellion, the new king sent him there to learn warfare under the expert tutelage of Harry Hotspur.

Henry is often remembered as Shakespeare's swaggering Prince Hal, consorting with ribald and vulgar companions to the shame of his royal father, who cannot help but compare his heir with the heir of the earl of Northumberland, the noble Henry Percy. But Shakespeare got everything about the youth of Henry V backward. Actually, Henry Percy belonged to Henry IV's generation—was three years older than Henry IV, in fact—and in this Welsh campaign he acted as elderly mentor to the boy.

When Henry was sixteen, Hotspur quit the campaign in disgust over lack of support, and the young prince of Wales took over the lead. At Shrewsbury in 1403, with the Percy family joining the Welsh in rebellion, Henry held the enemy forces at bay until his father could march to join him, whereupon they together defeated both rebel armies.

Like Hotspur's age, the character of Falstaff was an invention of Shakespeare. Far from roistering in taverns, the young prince of Wales spent much of his youth chairing his father's council, helping his increasingly ill father to govern the kingdom. Rigidly orthodox and narrow in religion, he patronized the campaign against Lollardy (an early form of Protestantism) and watched heretics burn for their beliefs. One such heretic, Sir John Oldcastle, had been a skilled and devoted soldier under Henry in Wales, and it is thought that it is his character that Shakespeare transformed into the debauched Falstaff. Shakespeare wrote good theater but not good history.

In 1413 Henry V inherited a crown and a guilty conscience. In spite of his guilt over Richard II's death, Henry IV hadn't been able to part with the crown that wasn't rightfully his, and had turned to self-reproach and hypochondria as poor seconds. Henry V couldn't part with his power either, but he dealt with it differently.

First, he had Richard II's body moved with great honor and pomp to Westminster Abbey, perhaps out of respect and affection for his early patron. Then he set out to make himself such a national hero that the English would forget how he came to be king. And they did forget, at least for his lifetime.

The one most effective way to unite a country behind its leader is a popular war, and England's new twenty-six-year-old king realized it. Henry chose to reignite the Hundred Years' War against France, because the English were never really happy unless they were fighting France. It was a fortuitous time because the French were suffering a deadly internal turmoil. The king of France, Charles VI, had been a contemporary of Richard II. Like Richard he came to the throne as a boy and suffered humiliating difficulties with royal uncles. Also like Richard, his reason had begun to fail. But Charles had lived longer, and by the time Henry V came to the throne, Charles was quite insane most of the time. He had brief spells of normalcy, when he was both sensitive and sensible, but the intervals were widely spaced and unpredictable.

Charles's wife was Isabeau of Bavaria, an aging beauty who was having an open affair with the duke of Burgundy, the most powerful noble in France. Isabeau and Burgundy were running France in the place of the king and wanted to keep it that way. The obstacle was the Dauphin (the traditional title for the eldest son of a French king), a vicious young man with the foresight of a lemming.

Other children had been born to Charles and Isabeau, the oldest daughter being Isabelle, who had been the child bride of Richard II. Henry had had a crush on Isabelle when he was a child and had wanted to marry her, but the little girl had absolutely refused to marry the son of the man who dethroned her husband. She had left England and later married someone else.

The next daughter of Charles and Isabeau was Maria, who became a nun, and the youngest was Katherine, who was born in 1401. She was destined to play a greater role in the English succession than Henry.

Isabeau ignored her husband and children. Charles VI and the little girls were kept in a large dirty castle where they existed on what was left from the servants' table. It was said they didn't even own a change of underwear. Such was the condition of France and the royal family when Henry decided to renew the English claim to the French throne.

As soon as he could assemble troops, Henry set out for France. Since he couldn't marry the oldest daughter, he had requested the hand of the youngest and had been refused. This had added fuel to the fire of English indignation.

The most famous battle of that war, in fact one of the

most famous battles in England's history, was at Agincourt on October 25, 1415. Henry's troops were vastly outnumbered, but they fought with the strength that sometimes comes of utter desperation. They also had the advantageous position and a leader whom they regarded with doglike devotion. The English fought like organized animals; the French troops fell all over one another in confusion. By the end of the day, the field looked like a slaughterhouse.

One casualty figure lists fifteen hundred French knights and five thousand French soldiers killed, but fewer than three hundred Englishmen. While such disparate figures represent only a guess, it was clear that Henry was the winner. Obviously France couldn't keep losing men at that rate. Henry's troops kept hacking their way farther and farther into the heart of the country, and finally, in May of 1420, France, in the person of Isabeau, gave up.

An agreement, called the Treaty of Troyes, was then reached and drawn up. According to the treaty, Charles VI was to remain king for the duration of his lifetime, which certainly wouldn't be long. Henry was to marry Katherine (Isabeau had dug her out of the castle and cleaned her up by then), and the Dauphin was disinherited so that Henry and his progeny could rule France.

The only person who didn't subscribe to the conditions of the treaty was the Dauphin. Katherine was delighted. Not only was she in love with this handsome prince, but the alternative would probably have been a return to hand-me-downs and table scraps.

Henry and Katherine, who, in spite of her upbringing, had become a beautiful, sophisticated young woman, were married in June, 1420. They had only two days together before Henry dashed off to settle some difficulties the

Dauphin was stirring up, and Katherine was temporarily returned to the "care" of her mother. Henry and his bride finally got back to England in February, 1421. He was welcomed with enormous enthusiasm. He had succeeded in making a national hero of himself.

No one gave a thought to the fact that Henry had had no business interfering with the affairs of France in the first place. Parliament even granted him the money to go back and round up the troublesome Dauphin, who was still at large. Henry left in August, and this time Katherine stayed behind in England. She was pregnant.

On December 6, 1421, Katherine gave birth to a son christened (naturally!) Henry. At the same time Henry and most of his troops had contracted dysentery. Henry kept after the Dauphin, but couldn't regain his health. Finally, the following August, he became too weak to go on, and at the age of thirty-five, he died, leaving England with a new king, a nine-month-old baby.

Henry had reigned only nine years and had spent almost the entire time in France. Like Richard the Lionhearted, he had maintained his heroic proportions by keeping a distance from his subjects and by dying before his glory became tarnished. Edward I and Edward III had been heroes in their youth too, but they had outlived their victories. Young warrior kings who die in their prime are the ones who are most revered.

Katherine turned her son over to a new generation of royal uncles and retired to live quietly. She did not wish to return to France, but she had no real place in English affairs. Little was heard of her until four years later, when she began to develop a scandalous bulge in her midsection. It seems there was a gentleman in charge of the wardrobe in her household named Owen Tudor. He was from

Wales, and people called him "the dumb Welshman" because he couldn't speak understandable English. But he
and Katherine understood each other well enough, and
between 1426 and 1436 she gave birth to five little
Tudors.

By 1436, Katherine's legitimate son, Henry VI, and his
council decided that the affair had gone far enough, and
they locked Owen up. Katherine died a year later.

Although Henry VI had a fanatic devotion to religious
propriety, he was always generous to his illegitimate
siblings. He made Edmund, the oldest, earl of Richmond.
Edmund grew up to marry Margaret Beaufort, a remarkable lady, who was a descendant of John of Gaunt and
Katherine Swynford. Edmund and Margaret were the parents of Henry Tudor, who would put a stop to the Wars
of the Roses and an end to the Plantagenets.

Henry VI
1421–1471

SOMEONE once suggested to the Vatican that Henry
VI should be declared a saint. The reply from Rome was,
"Absolutely not. There has to be a line drawn somewhere
between saints and fools."

Henry would have made a devout and incorruptible
monk, but it was his misfortune, and everyone else's, that
he was born to be king of England. His heroic father died
when Henry was only nine months old, leaving him the
English crown. Two months later his maternal grandfather, Charles VI of France, died too, making the baby
king of France as well, at least in theory. It is ironic that

the one person most massively unsuited to rule anything should be the only man in history to be king of both France and England.

But the French claim was shaky at best. Henry VI had an uncle, the Dauphin, later known as Charles VII, who was the son of Charles VI. He felt he had a better claim than Henry to the French throne, as indeed he did. Charles had wide enough support to keep the English constantly engaged in fighting him off in order to maintain their foothold in France.

When Henry V died, the baby king and the country were put in the care of his father's brothers. John, duke of Bedford, was to be in charge of the war in France, and Humphrey, duke of Gloucester, was responsible for the care of the king and domestic matters. Like most such arrangements, it led to a great deal of bickering.

The war in France dragged on and on. The Dauphin seemed to be slowly losing when a young woman presented herself to him in 1429, claiming divine inspiration. Though most of Charles's advisers felt she was merely a deranged peasant (a common feature of any crisis), Charles was convinced, probably out of sheer lack of better alternatives, so he let Joan of Arc lead his armies.

With Joan at the head of the Dauphin's forces, they began to score victory after victory, and by July, Charles was able to march into the center of the English-held territory, and he was crowned at Rheims. Henry's uncles decided that Henry must be crowned too, so they dragged the eight-year-old boy away from his devotions to be crowned in Paris. Since French kings were traditionally crowned at Rheims, the ceremony in Paris didn't carry much weight.

A far more important event was the death in 1431 of

Joan of Arc. England's French ally, the duke of Burgundy (the son of the paramour of Queen Isabeau), had captured Joan and turned her over, for a price, to Henry's uncle, John of Bedford. John felt it was politically and spiritually expedient to get rid of her, and so she was condemned for witchcraft and burned at the stake. Young Henry VI was present to observe part of the questioning of Joan. Her death turned the tide of French opinion against the English. The duke of Burgundy, anxious to be on the winning side when it was over, threw his support to the Dauphin. This shift ensured Charles VI's victory, and the Hundred Years' War ground to a halt. The final blow to the English cause was the death of the duke of Bedford. John left a widow, Jacquetta of Luxembourg, whose subsequent remarriage would figure largely in the next reign.

Henry returned to England, and within a few years his character began to become apparent. He was so wrapped up in religion as to be completely unworldly. He believed wholeheartedly in his divine right to *rule,* but he didn't feel any political responsibility to *govern.* He spent all his time founding schools for religious education, praying, studying, and discussing religious issues. When these activities were interrupted for the affairs of state, he became irritated in his own mild way. Morally, he was a medieval Victorian. He became smugly self-righteous and critical of any display of nudity or earthy humor. Of course, his opinions on such matters were universally ignored.

Henry's inclination in any crisis was to pray and to encourage everyone to act peaceably and with love. He refused to condone the death of those who were convicted of treason against him. It was a good Christian philosophy but completely impractical. Still, it might have worked had Henry not married Margaret of Anjou. Of all the women available, she was, beyond any doubt, the very worst choice possible.

Margaret was the daughter of René of Anjou, who was the ruler of two countries, neither of which recognized him as such. But it didn't bother René. He painted and planned parties, and when he was locked up anywhere (he spent a good deal of time locked up), he just went on painting. But he and his iron-willed daughter were very close.

Everyone was agreed that the wishy-washy King Henry VI needed a wife of strong character, and Margaret seemed a good choice. She was intelligent, sophisticated, and attractive, everything that Henry was not. But Henry and his advisers had no way of knowing that this fifteen-year-old girl would grow up to overwhelm Henry and his court with her arrogance and ambition.

The main drawback to Margaret at the time of the marriage (1445) was money. Margaret had none. René wasn't the sort of person to put away nest eggs for his daughters' dowries. Henry wasn't much better off financially. Losing the war in France had been expensive, so he was persuaded to pawn some of his jewels to pay a dressmaker to meet Margaret when she landed in England and whip up a suitable wardrobe for a queen.

Margaret never confided in anyone what she thought of Henry, but it's not hard to guess. Henry wore long dark coats over rough clothing with farmer's boots, because he regarding attractive clothing as one of the sins of the flesh, although he didn't object to Margaret's new finery (he never had the nerve to object to anything that Margaret did). His conversation was limited to religious matters and couldn't have been especially stimulating because his mentality was as meager and ordinary as his wardrobe.

At about this time, the activities of a royal cousin began to become important. Richard of York was the descendant of the second oldest of Edward III's sons. Henry was the descendant of the third oldest son of Edward III, so, according to the family tree, Richard of York was the rightful king. However, Henry's father and grandfather had both been kings, so no one, least of all Richard, was about to dispute his right.

No one took any interest in Richard's possible claim until Margaret came on the scene. She alone saw Richard as a menace to Henry's position. Richard was a capable, intelligent, and energetic man, and had replaced John of Bedford in trying to hang on to France. Margaret had taken over making Henry's decisions for him—a system that Henry found entirely satisfactory—and she decided to get Richard of York out of the limelight. She saw to it that he was sent to Ireland to serve for ten years. It was obviously just a means of getting him out of the way, and Richard recognized it as such, but rather than get into a losing battle with Margaret, he went in 1449.

Richard's entire family went along, including his wife, Cecily Neville, who was the youngest of the twenty-three children of the earl of Westmorland. Their two sons, Edward (later Edward IV), age seven in 1449, and Edmund, age six, went along too, as did three younger daughters. Two more sons would be born to Richard and Cecily: George of Clarence and Richard of Gloucester, who would be the last Plantagenet king.

Within a year of York's departure, a rebellion broke out in England. Had there been anyone sensible in charge, it could have been dealt with, but Henry's response to trouble was to retire to a quiet corner and pray. Margaret's opinions, which weren't worth much officially, were ignored.

Henry's council realized that the one person who could straighten matters out was Richard of York, and they prevailed upon him to return to England. Since nobody listened to Margaret's objections to the plan, she hired someone to assassinate Richard along the way. However, her employee bungled the job, and Richard returned intact. He made no attempt to dethrone Henry (as he could have done), but simply demanded an important place in the council. This was done.

Henry's worst troubles were just beginning. One of Margaret's staunchest supporters was Edmund Beaufort, duke of Somerset, a grandson of John of Gaunt through his third marriage. Henry IV had declared his half brothers ineligible for the throne, but Somerset saw it differently. He considered himself heir to the throne if Margaret had no children, and after six years of marriage without issue that began to look like a possibility. Naturally, Richard of York, who had a better claim in the first place than Henry, felt strongly that *he* should be Henry's heir. Henry just prayed.

The question of heirs was temporarily set aside in 1453, an eventful year. Up until then, Henry had simply been oppressively dull; in July, he went mad. He had apparently inherited the seed of insanity from his French grandfather. He sank into a lethargic state bordering on unconsciousness. He didn't eat or talk or even seem to hear or recognize anyone. He didn't even pray.

Henry was still in the vegetable state in October when a newborn baby named Edward was brought to him. But he neither understood nor cared that the child was his long-awaited son and heir. Margaret was frantic. She had been sure that the sight of their child would jar his feeble brain back on the track, but by March of 1454, it looked as though Henry's madness were permanent. Someone would have to be made responsible for the heir and the government.

Margaret had expected to fill that position herself and was furious when Parliament appointed her long-time enemy, Richard of York, as protector of the realm. Things stood that way until December, when Henry suddenly regained his senses, such as they were, and resumed praying. The power in England shifted back to Margaret and Somerset, but everyone was preparing for a return of Henry's insanity, which was inevitable.

York went home to confer with his advisers. Chief among them was the son of one of Cecily's brothers, Richard Neville, the earl of Warwick. Warwick was to play one of the most important roles in the Wars of the Roses and earn the resounding title of "Kingmaker." He and York assembled a good-sized army, then demanded that Henry admit that Somerset was a traitor and a general bad influence and turn him over to them. Actually, they meant Somerset *and* the queen, but didn't dare say so.

Henry, being completely under Margaret's thumb, refused. The York forces started moving toward London. The Lancaster forces started moving out. They accidentally met at the town of St. Albans.

The rivalries that caused the Wars of the Roses had been simmering for over half a century, and finally, in May of 1455, the first actual battle was fought at St. Albans. Henry was forced into a suit of armor, but he just sat in his tent and prayed. Even with that limited activity, he got a slight wound in the neck. Somerset was killed. York's forces won, but great losses occurred on both sides. The losses were not commoners, as was usual in war, but the nobility. That is the one feature that makes the Wars of the Roses unique.

Richard of York then went to Henry and again, instead of seizing his throne, tried to make peace. They patched things up, and that might have been the end of it but for Margaret. She was even more deranged than ever on the subject of Richard of York, now that she had a son whose claim to the throne she had to protect.

The balance of power between Margaret and Richard swung back and forth for years, as did Henry's sanity. Finally, by 1460, York succeeded in driving Margaret and her son into hiding. At long last he decided to announce his claim to the throne.

Henry was shocked. Apparently it had never occurred to him that such a thing might happen. The blame for this can be laid squarely at Margaret of Anjou's feet. If she hadn't kept harping on Richard's superior claims and about how he was trying to usurp the throne, he probably would not have thought of doing it.

No one was willing to take the responsibility for dethroning gentle, crazy Henry, and finally Parliament agreed to let him reign for the rest of his life. Thereafter, Richard and his heirs were to inherit the crown. This compromise suited everyone but Margaret, the mother tiger. She was not going to see her son Edward, the light of her life, cast off.

At the battle of Wakefield, Richard of York was killed. On the last day of 1460, Cecily Neville lost her husband, her brother (Warwick's father), and her son Edmund. Margaret marched toward London to rescue her pitiful husband from Warwick's care, and again the armies met at St. Albans. This time Margaret's Lancaster forces won.

Of course, Margaret hadn't eliminated the Yorkist claim; she had only driven it into the next generation. Richard of York's eighteen-year-old son Edward did not possess his father's patience. When he heard of his father's fate, he just marched into London (the Londoners hated Margaret and wouldn't let her in) and declared himself king. Richard of York could have done the same thing half a dozen times, but he hadn't. Edward simply took what he wanted. He then chased Margaret and Henry into hiding in Scotland. Eventually, Margaret ended up in France and Henry was captured and put in the Tower.

The Lancasters were to have one more try at the crown, but the fates of Margaret, Henry, and their son were in the hands of Edward IV and his Kingmaker.

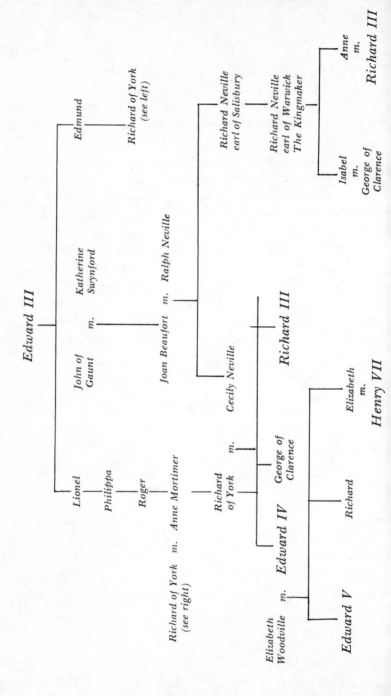

The White Rose—the York Claim

CHAPTER VI

The Roses-White

Edward IV
1442–1483

THE young man who proclaimed himself king in 1461 was a total contrast to Henry VI. Edward IV was huge, well over six feet tall and of strong build. He was universally considered to be devastatingly handsome, though surviving portraits make one wonder at medieval standards of male beauty. He had been in the thick of the Lancaster-York feud since the age of ten, when he ably commanded his father's armies in his absence. He was an enormously sexual man with an earthy, easygoing personality.

When Edward IV was crowned in June 1461, Margaret and Henry VI were slinking around in Scotland and the northern parts of England. Margaret would not give up. Repeated bloody defeats didn't deter her a bit. After all, the lives being lost were the English nobility, and she didn't care what happened to them—or to anybody—so long as she and her son survived to fight again. She kept gathering troops and starting rebellions, and Edward kept crushing them.

Margaret finally mislaid Henry during a retreat and

ended up in Burgundy (France) with her son. After that Henry meandered around in northern woods and towns for two years with a devoted handful of retainers. He was finally captured in 1465 and brought by Warwick's men to London. Warwick had Henry tied to a puny horse and exhibited him thus all the way to London. Once Edward found this out, he saw to it that Henry was treated as an honored prisoner. Edward himself had no desire to humiliate the former king. Henry was a nice man; even his enemies found it hard really to dislike him. All he ever inspired was indifference.

During all the turmoil of these first years of his reign, Edward found relaxation in hunting. One day while hunting in the forests of one of his favorite attendants, Antony Woodville, they came upon an artfully posed picnic scene. There, under a large oak tree, was Antony's widowed sister Elizabeth and her two baby sons. Edward was enchanted with Elizabeth, which was what she had hoped. But who were these Woodvilles?

During the early part of Henry VI's reign, his uncle, John of Bedford, had died leaving a handsome, spirited widow, Jacquetta of Luxembourg. She was escorted to England after John's death by a young knight of his household named Sir Richard Woodville. She (a princess of royal birth) and Richard (an unimportant knight) fell in love and married secretly. When Parliament found out, they were enraged, but it was too late to do anything about it. They gave Woodville a suitable rank, and he became Lord Rivers. Richard and Jacquetta settled down to raising a large family. The oldest child was Elizabeth, the charming lady of the picnic scene. She had been married to Sir John Grey, who had died fighting on the Lancastrian side at the second battle of St. Albans.

Sir John's lands had then been seized by Edward, and now Lady Grey was waiting under the oak tree to apply all her charms to recovering her sons' inheritance.

Edward was determined to make this lady his mistress. She was five years his senior and a ripe beauty. There ensued several romantic, secret picnics under the oak tree (without the children), and Elizabeth is said to have told Edward, "While I'm not good enough to be your wife, I'm far too good to be your mistress." A pretty line, which accomplished what she undoubtedly intended.

After months of agonizing search for some third alternative, Edward realized he couldn't get Elizabeth to bed without marrying her. He was staying at a manor near the Woodville home, Grafton Regis, on the night of April 30, 1464. He rose before dawn, saying that he couldn't sleep and was going hunting alone. He quickly slipped over to the Woodville home, and by prearrangement, he and Elizabeth were secretly married in the presence of Jacquetta and two gentlewomen witnesses. Not even Lord Rivers and Antony were let in on the secret. Edward returned later to his host's home for breakfast, where his companions wondered why three hours of hunting had made him so tired and happy.

Though his councillors had all been nagging Edward to marry, they would never have approved this marriage if they had known about it. While marrying an English woman might be a popular move, no English king had ever married less than a royal princess. The Woodvilles weren't commoners, but they were certainly considered minor nobility in spite of the blue blood in the headstrong Jacquetta's veins. More than that, they were heartily disliked. They were a large family, Elizabeth and Antony being the oldest of thirteen children, who were beautiful, educated, talented, and intensely loyal to one another. Like Edward, they were quick-witted but easy-going and luxury prone, and they had all been on the losing Lancastrian side until Edward took the crown, at which time they swung over in a body to the Yorkist standard. For that reason Edward kept his marriage a secret for several months.

By this stage of Edward's reign, Warwick was beginning to get out of hand. Since he was largely responsible for helping Edward get and hold the crown, he liked to think of himself as the real ruler and of Edward as a mere figurehead. Accordingly, a quiet battle of wills went on between Warwick and Edward. Edward was not cut out to be a puppet king. He was a superb general whose troops considered him a leader and a friend. He understood the nuances of politics and diplomacy and the theory and detail of trade and economy. He was, in fact, a very well-rounded ruler. These things Warwick could not or would not acknowledge.

The Kingmaker also took it upon himself to start bargaining for royal princesses. But if Edward had never met Elizabeth, it is doubtful that he would have married a foreign princess. His policy was to avoid international entanglements of any kind for fear of getting involved in a foreign war before the domestic wars were straightened out.

However, Warwick was undeterred by Edward's opinions and set out to make a match between Edward and a certain Lady Bona, whose sister was the queen of France. Warwick was at the French court making the arrangements for the wedding when Edward went on his early morning hunt to Grafton Regis.

Warwick returned to England full of plans for the

French marriage, but Edward kept thinking of excuses for putting it off. Finally, at a meeting of the council in September, Edward was forced to commit himself. He said he thought he should marry one of his countrywomen and that he had, in fact, done so five months before.

Warwick was furious. Not only had Edward gone against his wishes, he had also made a fool of him, publicly, internationally. The Kingmaker went off to sulk over this insult and determine how to get Edward under his control.

Warwick decided against an open break at first, but began to nurse along a variety of intrigues that would come of age in a few years' time. In the meanwhile, he and the rest of the older nobility grew wary of the Woodvilles. The upstart royal in-laws were rapidly gobbling up important titles and positions. It was logical that they do so, of course, for the Wars of the Roses had taken a terrific toll of the old nobility, and the Woodvilles were well suited to fill the gaps. Lord Rivers, Elizabeth's father, became Earl Rivers and was made constable of England. Her brother Antony became Lord Scales, and was Edward's trusted confidant. Elizabeth's oldest son of her first marriage was given a title, and her younger brothers became bishops, admirals, and knights. Her sisters had good matches made for them, as did her brother John, who scandalized the court by marrying an extremely wealthy eighty-year-old duchess. John wasn't yet twenty.

By 1469, it was obvious that the Nevilles, Warwick in particular, had lost their hold over the handsome young king. Edward was grateful for their help but would never be Warwick's pawn. Just the same, Warwick's nickname of "Kingmaker" had gone to his head. The answer to his problem was simple: since he couldn't control the king, he would *replace* him with someone more pliable. There were two good candidates at hand. Edward IV had a younger brother George, duke of Clarence, a slimy boy who was altogether willing to replace his brother. He was vain and treacherous and sufficiently stupid for Warwick to lead him around by his haughty nose.

The first step in the Clarence plan involved getting Clarence married to Isabel Neville, one of Warwick's daughters. Edward forbade the marriage, but it was performed secretly. That way, Warwick's new pawn also became his son-in-law.

Even Warwick could see that Clarence wasn't exactly a bargain, so he needed to have a stand-by ready. It occurred to him that there was still an ex-king extant, and *he* was about the most pliable person alive. But Henry VI was by nature and circumstance a poor ally. He was still locked up in the Tower and certainly wouldn't lift a finger to help himself. If Warwick wanted to make a figurehead of Henry, he would simply *have* to deal with Margaret. However, Margaret's long suit was holding grudges, and she hated no one on earth more than Warwick. While she would have sold her soul to give her son a chance at the throne, it looked unlikely that she could be persuaded to team up with Warwick.

He too had plenty of pride, enough to spare, but he went to France to see Margaret and finally won her over by, quite literally, begging on hands and knees. Moreover, he arranged for a betrothal between Margaret's son, Prince Edward, who was living in France with his mother, and Anne Neville, another of Warwick's daughters.

Poor Anne. Betrothal to that nasty adolescent was just the first tragedy in her short, sad life. But remember her. She will be an important figure in another reign.

Warwick was now ready to put somebody on the English throne, and he had arranged to be a close relative to whoever it was. He landed in England in September of 1470 and managed with a combination of luck and skill to take King Edward by surprise. But Edward wasn't captured. He fled to the court of Charles of Burgundy, who was married to Edward's sister Margaret. Meanwhile, Queen Elizabeth Woodville had gone into sanctuary in England with her three daughters and Jacquetta. Six weeks later, she gave birth to the long-awaited male heir, the future Edward V.

Warwick, with his lieutenants, Clarence and Jasper Tudor (Henry VI's half-brother), marched into London to trot Henry out of the Tower and dust him off for a new reign. Queen Margaret, for once, had not dashed into the fray. She was still in France, waiting to see how things were going to go.

It took Edward only five months to gather his wits and his troops and return. He was met with neither enthusiasm nor hostility in most places. The common people were sick and tired of the Wars of the Roses. They didn't care much who won, so long as the warring nobles would stop using their pastures for battlefields.

But Edward did gain some support, chiefly from Clarence, who had finally caught on that Warwick wasn't being entirely honest with him. The York armies and the Warwick armies met at Barnet in April of 1471 and Edward was victorious. The Kingmaker was among the dead.

Margaret had finally arrived in England by that time. Therefore, hard on the heels of his victory at Barnet, Edward had to contend with her forces at Tewkesbury. Although it wasn't as spectacular a battle as Barnet, Tewkesbury was a more thorough victory for Edward, because it was there that Prince Edward was killed and Margaret was captured. She was taken to the Tower to join Henry VI, who died the day she arrived, May 24, 1471. He was probably murdered, though it has never been proved.

There was no longer an extra king of England or any disputed heirs. There were no longer any legitimate Lancasters. The Wars of the Roses were officially over, though the royal bloodshed would continue for some time. Queen Margaret gave up at long last. She was shuttled around to various castles for a time, and eventually sent back to her father, René, who was still painting. She retired quietly with a lifetime of bitter memories and died in August of 1482.

Edward was now undisputed king of England, and free to get fat and lazy. He was also able to give all his attention to his drinking and to his sex life. He was fond of his English merchants, their wool, and their wives. Queen Elizabeth seemed to accept his mistresses without much regret. She had provided him with ten children, three of whom were important to history.

The only other excitement during the remainder of Edward's reign involved Clarence. When Isabel Neville and their baby died suddenly in 1477, Clarence went berserk. After he had killed a few people, he was brought to trial and found guilty. Edward couldn't bring himself to put aside the verdict because Clarence was a national menace, but he couldn't allow a public execution either. Just the same, Clarence was executed, and the story was that Edward permitted him to choose the means of death himself. Clarence chose to be drowned in a barrel of very expensive wine. Whether true or not, it made a good story and a suitable ending for Clarence.

In April of 1483, Edward IV, age forty, fat, sloppy, and alcoholic, complained of abdominal pains. Ten days later he was dead, probably of a ruptured appendix. He left a son, Edward V, whose fate would be one of history's most hotly debated mysteries.

Edward V
1470–1483 (?)

EDWARD V was born November 1, 1470, at Westminster, where his mother was hiding from the Kingmaker. The circumstances of his birth are well known; the circumstances of his death are not. For almost five hundred years men have argued hotly and passionately about the fate of this boy.

Much is known about the first twelve years of his life, none of it especially revealing. Edward IV had a fine castle built in the Welsh Marches for his young heir. The boy was sent to Ludlow Castle, where his mother's brother Antony Woodville was in charge of the household. His days were rigidly supervised according to an educational schedule that Edward IV had outlined, and he was subjected to big doses of religion and literature.

Young Edward's sheltered academic life abruptly fell apart on April 9, 1483, when Edward IV died unexpectedly. The twelve-year-old scholar was suddenly king of England.

Naturally, his mother and her relatives, the Woodvilles, who had held much power in the previous reign, intended to continue to hold the reins of government for the little boy. But without the protection of Edward IV they were unable to do so. They had risen too far, too fast, and were universally hated. The little boy's paternal uncle, Richard, duke of Gloucester, was appointed protector, an arrangement that had been specified in the late king's will.

When Elizabeth Woodville heard that Richard of Gloucester had taken control of the child when he went to escort him on his journey to London, she gathered her household, hitched up her skirts, and again bolted for sanctuary. She, her daughters, and her younger son, a nine-year-old also named Richard, were in hiding when the young King Edward and his Uncle Richard reached London on the fourth of May, 1483. The date for young Edward V's coronation was set for June 22.

How was the boy reacting to all this political juggling? Well, mostly he cried. It seems that every time there was an argument within his range, he wept. The rest of the time he pouted or sat around looking wistful and sad.

Edward IV appears to have made a mistake common to loving fathers. He was determined that his child should not suffer the same harsh life that he, the father, had endured. The result of such an attitude is that the child often grows up to be pampered, naive, or spineless, because the adverse conditions that formed the character of the father are unavailable to the child. This is possibly being unduly critical of the boy king, because no one knows what he might have grown into, but when one considers how much earlier children matured in the fifteenth century, it is difficult to have much faith in a sniveling twelve-year-old.

In the middle of June it was revealed that the young king's father, Edward IV, had once been betrothed to a lady named Eleanor Butler. As mentioned before, a betrothal was a binding legal contract, and certain legal steps had to be taken to break such a contract. According to Gloucester, the betrothal had not been broken at the time of Edward IV's marriage to Elizabeth Woodville and that made the king's marriage illegal. As a consequence, the boy, Edward V—in fact, all the children of Edward IV— was illegitimate, and Richard of Gloucester, Edward IV's next-of-legitimate-kin, was king of England.

The coronation plans went ahead but with a new central figure. The person crowned was not the boy, Edward V, but his uncle, Richard III.

Strangely enough, Elizabeth Woodville decided to come out of sanctuary about this time, and she turned her younger boy over to the new king to be lodged in the Tower with his brother. The boys were seen occasionally at the windows, waving to the busy throng that always surrounded the Tower. Then, gradually, they were seen less often, and by the next year they were not seen at all.

What happened to them? No one knows. For centuries historians have stated positively that Richard III, their uncle, had them killed. Yet years later young men turned up claiming they were the missing princes.

Richard III
1452–1485

T UDOR historians, writing for the family of the man who took Richard III's life and throne, say that Richard III was born with long hair and teeth. They describe him as small, dark, and ugly, with a shriveled arm and a hunchback. They say his soul was as sinister as his appearance.

Many twentieth-century history books also state without

reservation that Richard III murdered his brother's children. But anyone who sees the portrait of Richard III
(painted during his short reign) cannot help but wonder
about these stories. The portrait shows a well-proportioned
man with features that are fine, regular, and rather handsome. It isn't the face of the former huge, glittering Plantagenets, like Edward IV, but neither is it the face of a
deformed monster.

Somewhere between that thoughtful face in the portrait
and the tormented sinner in Shakespeare's *Richard III*
lies the truth about this king. Let us begin with the facts
that are *not* disputed. Richard was the youngest son of
Richard of York and Cecily Neville and was born on
October 2, 1452, at Fotheringay Castle. As a child, he
developed a tremendous devotion to his older brother
Edward, who made himself Edward IV when Richard was
only nine years old. Edward was young Richard's idol,
and in 1470, when Warwick the Kingmaker chased Edward
into exile, Richard was by Edward's side. At the age of
eighteen he was the moving force in organizing Edward's
return to power.

Richard spent most of the rest of Edward's reign keep-
the north of England in check. This was no small matter,
for the bulk of Edward's power and popularity was in
London. The northern part of England was pro-Lan-
castrian. Richard was not only successful in controlling
this rebellious territory, he was popular there.

The only notable event during these years was his
marriage. During his youth Richard had been on good
terms with his cousin Warwick's family, including Warwick's daughters, Isabel and Anne Neville. Isabel had
married the scoundrel in Richard's family, his brother
George, duke of Clarence (the character who ended his

days in a barrel of wine). Warwick's younger daughter Anne had been betrothed to Edward, the son of the dispossessed Henry VI. Richard was fond of his cousin Anne, who was two years younger than he, and when Prince Edward died at Tewkesbury, Richard wanted to marry Anne.

Richard's big brother Clarence had other ideas. Edward IV had seized the Warwick holdings, and Clarence had high hopes that Edward would turn the whole bundle over to him. But if Richard married the other Neville girl, naturally Edward could be expected to divide Warwick's holdings between Clarence and Richard. Clarence was not of a sharing disposition. He whisked the girl to his castle out of sight, and Richard finally found her disguised as a kitchen servant in London.

This incident is a shining example of the kind of interpretative heyday historians can have with a few facts. The Tudor writers, contentedly gnawing away at Richard's character, assured posterity that the girl was hiding from Richard. They explain with confidence that the girl was terrified at the thought of marrying the monstrous hunchback. But why should she hide from Richard? He couldn't have forced her out of Clarence's protection, had she wanted protection. Knowing Clarence's character, one finds it far more logical to assume that Anne was hiding from Clarence. Indeed, about the only way Richard could have discovered her among the pots and pans was by her sending word to him. Whichever interpretation you prefer, Anne left the kitchens behind and married Richard in 1474. Later in the year their son was born.

We have seen in the chapter on Edward V the skeleton of what happened after the death of Edward IV, but it is necessary to look at the facts from Richard's point of view. His "usurpation" of his nephew's throne is based on the story of Edward's former and unbroken betrothal to Eleanor Butler, as told by Bishop Stillington, who had witnessed the pledge. The betrothal had all the makings of a good trumped-up excuse for deposing the child, except for one thing: it was probably true.

Edward IV had never distinguished himself by abiding by contracts, especially when women were involved. An unbroken betrothal may also explain why he kept his marriage to Elizabeth Woodville a secret for so long. Once they were married, no one could do anything about it except perhaps someone who knew about the other contract. Maybe the interval before the announcement was planned to give Edward a chance to talk things over with someone like Bishop Stillington.

Richard had other motives for seizing the crown. Even his admirers can't deny that ambition figured in his action, but the important thing from the standpoint of the nation was that boy kings were disastrous, especially boy kings in the clutches of greedy unpopular relatives. Everyone was frightened of the sort of things the Woodvilles might put Edward up to in their own interests. England needed an intelligent adult Plantagenet on the throne, and Richard fit the bill perfectly.

Richard was crowned with Anne and their son at his side on July 5, 1483. All three of them would die within the next two years. The child went first on March 31, 1484, at the age of nine. Anne and Richard weren't with him and didn't know that he was ill, except that he had always been delicate. Richard was grief-stricken, and Anne's health went steadily downhill from then on. She died almost a year later at the age of thirty-one. Anne was tubercular, but the Tudor version of her death says

Richard poisoned her to marry his niece, Edward IV's daughter Elizabeth. Of all the things that the Tudors claim about Richard III, the rumor about marrying his niece was the only one that actually got started during Richard's lifetime, and he wasted no time informing England that he had no intention of marrying Elizabeth.

Although the two young princes had disappeared, Elizabeth Woodville brought her daughters to court just the same, and was, by all accounts, having a gay time. Would this woman, who had a fanatic devotion to her family, have come out of sanctuary to live at Richard's court unless she was quite sure her beloved sons were safe?

And yet, what did happen to the boys? Richard came to the throne in the summer of 1483. By the following Easter the two boys, who had earlier been seen playing in the garden at the Tower, were seen and heard of no more.

When Henry Tudor ascended the throne after Richard's death, he brought an act of attainder against the dead king that charged him with having murdered Henry VI, with having murdered Henry's son Edward, with having poisoned his wife in order to marry his niece, and with having contrived the murder of his brother, the duke of Clarence—all pretty trumped-up accusations. What the act of attainder did *not* claim was that Richard had murdered the little princes in the Tower.

Shakespeare's account of Richard III is based largely on a Latin narrative written by—or found among the papers of—Sir Thomas More. No one knows where More got his information, but since he was the student of an unscrupulous man named Morton, who had been alive in Richard's day and despised him, it is a natural assumption that Morton was his source. But Morton and More were both in the service of the Tudor family, and hence their version of Richard's life is automatically suspect, for the Tudors had to blacken their predecessor's name in order to justify their own shaky claim to the English throne.

Did Richard have the boys murdered? If so, why didn't he bring out their smothered bodies and display them to the public as victims of "fever"? Did some overzealous supporter of Richard do away with them unknown to his master? Unlikely. Why perform such a service unless you profit from it, and there is no record of Richard rewarding anyone commensurate with such a deed. Perhaps Richard had the boys spirited away to safety in fear of this very thing. This would help to explain Elizabeth Woodville's return to court, if she were a party to the secret. This would also explain why the boys' deaths were not added to Henry's attainder—if they turned up some day safe and well, they would make a fool of him.

Perhaps someone rescued them, and in the escape one of them died. This is the story told by Perkin Warbeck in later years, and given the wishy-washy personality of the older boy, it is a possibility. It's true that Henry Tudor, though contemptuous of most pretenders to his throne (several young men turned up during his reign, claiming to be Edward V grown up or his brother Richard), was upset by Warbeck. He put him in the Tower and later had him executed.

However, speculation can never be anything more than that—perhapses. Unless some patient scholar turns up some dusty old record that explains the truth, we will never know more than that about this most fascinating mystery in the history of England.

By the summer of 1485 there was a far greater threat to Richard than rumors. Henry Tudor had decided to be king of England and was gathering troops to make good his ambitions. Henry was a sort of half brother to the Lancastrian line. His mother was a Beaufort, a descendant of John of Gaunt and Katherine Swynford, that couple whose children had been legitimatized but barred from the succession. Henry's father was Edmund Tudor, a descendant of Henry V's widow, Katherine of Valois, and her Welsh gentleman of the wardrobe, Owen Tudor. In other words, he had virtually no claim to the throne. About a dozen Plantagenets were in line in front of him, and most of them disappeared in short order during his reign.

Henry Tudor sailed from France, landed in Wales, and marched into England. Richard's forces met him at Bosworth field on August 22, 1485. When it appeared the Tudor forces were winning, Richard in desperation tried to race through the thick of battle to fight Henry personally. He was cut down before he got there. His crown (not the coronation model, but a light circlet for battle wear) landed in a bush from which the ever-frugal Henry retrieved it. Richard's body was stripped, thrown over a horse, and carted like a sack of flour to a nearby town for everyone to see. Two of the shortest reigns in English history had come to an end. And with them the rule of the Plantagenet family.

The Red Rose—the Lancaster-Tudor Claim

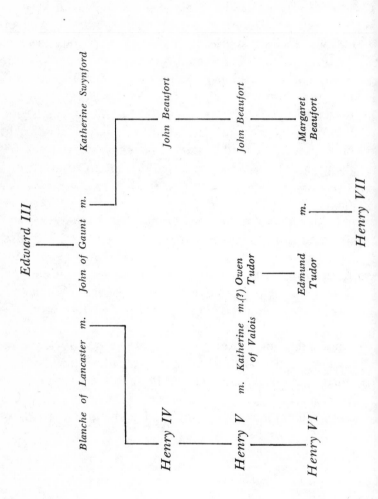

Epilog

So, that was the end of Plantagenet rule. This flashy, fascinating, all-too-human family would be succeeded on the English throne by the stingy Tudors, the obstinate Stuarts, and the plodding—but on the whole meritorious —Hanovers. But Plantagenet blood has not died out. By devious routes through the veins of various royal personages of many nationalities, it has come down to Queen Elizabeth II, who still displays the Plantagenet lions on her royal coat of arms.

Did the Plantagenets do England any good? Yes, although mostly by accident.

Richard I, trying to finance his Crusade, sold towns their charters of liberties—thus spurring the growth of commerce, industry, and middle-class-ness. King John, trying to squeeze out of a tight corner, sealed Magna Carta—thus admitting in writing that law must stand above even the power of a king. Edward I, needing money to make war on Scots and Welshmen, forced commoners to be represented in his Parliament—thus taking the first step toward a broad-based democracy. And the Yorks and Lancasters, squabbling over the throne, killed off Eng-

land's nobility—thus paving the way for a strong centra-
lized government under the Tudors and ultimately for
British nationhood.

Above all, the Plantagenets kept the peace at home.
Men did not ask much of a medieval king. They wanted
him to be just enough to settle their quarrels fairly, frugal
enough to make small demands on their slim purses,
knightly enough to champion the poor and the weak occasionally, pious enough to live equably with Mother
Church. But mostly they wanted him to be master in his
own house—strong enough to keep his marauding barons
in line. If he did that, he could carry war abroad to some
other land, and bring home glory, to his heart's content.

By and large—with some exceptions—this is what the
Plantagenets did. In 1485 the last of them left behind a
land that had known stability for five hundred years.

Bibliography

*Andrew, Prudence, *The Constant Star*. New York: G. P. Putnam's Sons, 1964. (Richard II.)

*_____ *Ordeal by Silence*. New York: G. P. Putnam's Sons, 1961. (Henry II.)

*_____ *A Question of Choice*. New York: G. P. Putnam's Sons, 1962. (Edward IV.)

Appleby, John T., *England Without Richard, 1189-1199*. Ithaca, N.Y.: Cornell University Press, 1965.

_____ *Henry II*. London: G. Bell & Sons, Ltd., 1962.

_____ *John, King of England*. New York: Alfred A. Knopf, Inc., 1959.

_____ *The Troubled Reign of King Stephen*. New York: Barnes and Noble, 1970.

*Barnes, Margaret Campbell, *Isabella the Fair*. Philadelphia: Macrae Smith Co., 1957. (Edward II.)

*_____ *The King's Bed*. Philadelphia: Macrae Smith Co., 1961. (Richard III.)

*_____ *The Tudor Rose*. Philadelphia: Macrae Smith Co., 1953. (Henry VII.)

*_____ *Within the Hollow Crown*. Philadelphia: Macrae Smith Co., 1947. (Richard II.)

*_____ *The Passionate Brood*. Philadelphia: Macrae Smith Co., 1945. (Henry II.)

Barton, John, and Law, Joyce, *The Hollow Crown*. New York: The Dial Press, 1971.

Bryant, Arthur, *The Story of England*. Boston: Houghton Mifflin Co., 1954.

*Bryher, Winifred, *The Fourteenth of October*. New York: Pantheon Books, 1952. (William I.)

_____ *This January Tale*. New York: Harcourt Brace & Co., 1966.

*Butler, Margaret, *The Lion of England*. New York: Coward, McCann and Geoghegan, 1973. (Henry II.)

*Charques, Dorothy, *Men Like Shadows*. New York: Coward, McCann, Inc., 1949. (Richard I.)

*Chidsey, Donald Barr, *This Bright Sword*. New York: Crown Publishers, Inc., 1957. (John.)

Churchill, Winston S., *A History of the English Speaking People.* Vol. I, *The Birth of Britain.* New York: Dodd, Mead and Co., 1956.

Clive, Mary, *This Sun of York.* New York: Alfred A. Knopf, 1974.

*Costain, Thomas B., *Below the Salt.* Garden City, N.Y.: Doubleday and Company, Inc., 1957. (John.)

_____ *The Conquerors.* Garden City, N.Y.: Doubleday and Co., 1949.

_____ *The Last Plantagenets.* Garden City, N.Y.: Doubleday and Co., Inc., 1962.

_____ *The Magnificent Century.* Garden City, N.Y.: Doubleday and Co., Inc., 1951.

_____ *The Three Edwards.* Garden City, N.Y.: Doubleday and Co., Inc., 1958.

Dale, Phillip Marshall, *Medical Biographies.* Norman, Okla.: University of Oklahoma Press, 1952.

*Duron, Maurice, *The She-Wolf of France.* New York: Charles Scribner's Sons, 1960. (Edward II.)

*Duggan, Alfred, *The Devil's Brood.* New York: Coward-McCann, Inc., 1949. (Henry II.)

*_____ *The Cunning of the Dove.* New York: Pantheon Books, 1960. (William I.)

*_____ *Leopards and Lilies.* New York: Coward-McCann, Inc., 1957. (John.)

Erickson, Arvel B., and Havran, Martin J., *England—Prehistory to the Present.* New York: Frederick A. Praeger, Inc., 1968.

Farrington, Robert, *The Killing of Richard III.* New York: Charles Scribner's Sons, 1971.

Freeman, Edward A., *The Reign of William Rufus.* 2 vols. London: Oxford University Press, 1882.

*Gerson, Noel, *The Conqueror's Wife.* Garden City, N.Y.: Doubleday and Co., Inc., 1957. (William I.)

Gervase, Mathew, *The Court of Richard III.* Garden City, N.Y.: Doubleday and Co., Inc., 1968.

*Greenberg, Joanne, *The King's Persons.* New York: Holt, Rinehart & Winston, 1963. (Richard I.)

Hamilton, Franklin, *Challenge for a Throne.* New York: The Dial Press, Inc., 1967.

Harvey, John, *The Plantagenets.* New York: The Macmillan Company, 1959.

*Harwood, Alice, *Merchant of the Ruby.* Indianapolis, Ind.: The Bobbs-Merrill Co., Inc., 1950. (Edward IV–Henry VII.)

*Hayraft, Molly Costain, *My Lord Brother the Lion Heart.* Philadelphia: J. B. Lippincott Co., 1945. (Richard I.)

*_____ *The Lady Royal.* Philadelphia: J. B. Lippincott Co., 1964. (Edward III.)

Henderson, Phillip, *Richard Coeur de Lion.* New York: W. W. Norton, 1959.

*Heyer, Georgette, *The Conqueror.* New York: E. P. Dutton & Co., Inc., 1966. (William I.)

Hibbert, Christopher, *The Court at Windsor*. New York: Harper & Row, Inc., 1964.

_____ *Tower of London*. New York: Newsweek Book Division, 1971.

*Holland, Cecelia, *The Firedrake*. New York: Atheneum, 1966. (William I.)

Hutchison, Harold, *Edward II*. New York: Stein and Day, 1971.

_____ *Henry V*. New York: John Day Co., 1967.

_____ *The Hollow Crown*. New York: John Day Co., 1961.

*Jackson, D. V. S., *Walk with Peril*. New York: G. P. Putnam's Sons, 1959. (Henry V.)

*Jarman, Rosemary, *We Speak No Treason*. Boston: Little, Brown & Co., Inc., 1971. (Richard III.)

* _____ *The King's Grey Mare*. Boston: Little, Brown & Co., Inc., 1973. (Edward IV.)

*Kelly, Amy, *Eleanor of Aquitaine and the Four Kings*. New York: Vintage Books, 1957. (Henry II, Richard I, John.)

Kendall, Paul Murray, *Richard III*. New York: W. W. Norton & Co., Inc., 1965.

_____ *The Yorkist Age*. New York: W. W. Norton & Co., Inc., 1962.

*Lewis, Hilda, *Harlot Queen*. New York: David McKay Co., Inc., 1970. (Edward II.)

* _____ *Wife to Henry V*. New York: G. P. Putnam's Sons, 1957.

* _____ *Wife to the Bastard*. New York: David McKay & Co., 1966. (William I.)

Lloyd, Alan, *The Making of a King, 1066*. New York: Holt, Rinehart & Winston, 1966.

*Lofts, Norah, *Eleanor the Queen*. Garden City, N.Y.: Doubleday and Co., Inc., 1951. (Henry II.)

* _____ *The Lute Player*. Garden City, N.Y.: Doubleday and Co., Inc., 1951. (Richard I.)

*Maiden, Cecil, *Harp into Battle*. New York: Thomas Y. Crowell Co., 1959. (John.)

Mancini, Dominic, *The Usurpation of Richard the Third*. London: Oxford University Press, 1969.

*Maughan, A. M. *Harry of Monmouth*. New York: William Sloane Associates, 1956. (Henry V.)

*Muntz, Hope, *The Golden Warrior*. New York: Charles Scribner's Sons, 1949. (William I.)

Murray, Jane, *The Kings and Queens of England*. New York: Charles Scribner's Sons, 1974.

*Mydans, Shelley, *Thomas*. Garden City, N.Y.: Doubleday and Co., Inc., 1965. (Henry II.)

Palmer, Marian, *The White Boar*. Garden City, N.Y.: Doubleday and Co., Inc., 1968. (Richard III.)

_____ *The Wrong Plantagenet*. Garden City, N.Y.: Doubleday and Co., Inc., 1972. (Henry VII.)

*Pargeter, Edith, *The Bloody Field*. New York: The Viking Press, 1972. (Henry V.)

Pernoud, Régine, *Eleanor of Aquitaine*. New York: Coward-McCann, Inc., 1968

*Potter, Jeremy, *A Trail of Blood*. New York: McCall Publishing Co., 1970. (Edward V.)

*Powers, Anne, *Ride East! Ride West!* New York: The Bobbs Merrill Co., 1947. (Edward III.)

*Rofheart, Martha, *Fortune Made His Sword*. New York: G. P. Putnam's Sons, 1972. (Henry V.)

*Seton, Anya, *Katherine*. Boston: Houghton Mifflin Co., 1953. (Edward III–Richard II.)

Simons, Eric N., *The Reign of Edward IV*. New York: Barnes and Noble, Inc., 1966.

Strickland, Agnes, *Lives of the Bachelor Kings of England*. London: Simkin, Marshall & Co., 1861.

_____ *Lives of the Queens of England*. London: G. Bell & Sons, 1885.

*Stubbs, Jean, *An Unknown Welshman*. New York: Stein and Day, 1972. (Henry VII.)

*Tey, Josephine, *The Daughter of Time*. New York: The Macmillan Company, 1951. (Edward V–Richard III.)

Usherwood, Stephen, *Reign by Reign*. New York: W. W. Norton, Inc., 1960.

*Vidal, Gore, *A Search for the King*. New York: E. P. Dutton and Co., Inc., 1950. (Richard I.)

Warren, W. L., *King John*. New York: W. W. Norton, 1961.

*Westcott, Jan, *The White Rose*. New York: G. P. Putnam's Sons, 1969. (Edward IV.)

White, R. J., *A Short History of England*. New York: Cambridge University Press, 1967.

*Williams, Jay, *Tomorrow's Fire*. New York: Atheneum, 1964. (Richard I.)

*Historical fiction.

INDEX

religious zeal of, 103
and Richard II, relationship of, 102, 103
succession arrangement with France, 105
Henry VI
  birth of, 106
  coronation in France, 108
  death of, 124
  imprisonment of, 116, 118
  insanity of, 112
  intelligence of, 107
  as King of France, 107
  marriage to Margaret of Anjou, 110
  money problems of, 110
  rebellion against, 111
  regents of, 108
  religion of, 109
  son of, 112
  succession agreement of, 114
Henry VII
  accusations against Richard III, 131
  claim to throne, 132, 133
Hotspur, Harry, 102. *See also* Percy, Henry.
House of Commons, 63
House of Lords, 63
Hugh de Lusignan
  betrothal to Isabelle of Angoulême, 48
  capture of, 50
  marriage to Isabelle of Angoulême, 54, 58
Humphrey of Gloucester, 108
Hundred Years' War
  end of, 109
  and Henry V, 103
  start of, 80